The Greater Way of Freedom

Dictations of the Ascended Masters
Given to the Messenger Elizabeth Clare Prophet

Summit University  Press

A Summit Lighthouse Publication
Colorado Springs

The Greater Way of Freedom
Published by
THE SUMMIT LIGHTHOUSE, INC.
Box A
Colorado Springs, Colorado 80901

Copyright © 1976 by The Summit Lighthouse, Inc.

LIBRARY OF CONGRESS CATALOG CARD NUMBER: 76-7636

INTERNATIONAL STANDARD BOOK NUMBER: 0-916766-14-4

Printed in the United States of America

Summit University Press
First Printing

Freedom is a flame. It cannot be confined to the realm of politics, or religion, or philosophy. It encompasses all. Burning within the hearts of men and nations can be found the unquenchable fires of freedom. Throughout the centuries seekers have discovered the way of freedom, the freedom of which Jesus spoke when he said, "Ye shall know the truth, and the truth shall make you free."

In the first century A.D., the Greek philosopher Epictetus made the profound observation "No man is free who is not the master of himself." Therein lies the key to freedom; for only when man, by the correct use of free will, has risen in consciousness and thereby developed self-mastery can he truly be free from the bondage and the subtle obstacles that have shackled him to a fruitless existence.

You may say to yourself, "This is all well and good, but such mastery is beyond my capabilities." Perhaps you need assistance. There are teachers—the ascended masters. Lao-Tse, Buddha, Maitreya, Confucius, Jesus, and Saint Francis are but a few of the saints and sages who have risen from every kindred, tongue, and people to attain liberation and reunion with God. They have been working for thousands of years, and they continue to work with earnest seekers who have made the greater way of freedom their goal.

If you will receive them, the masters lovingly offer guidance and instruction. Having reached the summit to which we now climb, they are releasing teachings that, when applied, lead to self-mastery and the freedom of the soul in God.

The Greater Way of Freedom contains the transcription of dictations from the ascended masters given through their appointed representative Elizabeth Clare Prophet in a two-day seminar in Washington, D.C., together with the dictations by Saint Germain and Sanat Kumara given in Anaheim, California, and Colorado Springs, Colorado. Also included is the text of Saint Germain's dedication of the Rakoczy Mansion in Washington, D.C.

In reading these dictations, may you experience the blessing of freedom's flame that was bestowed upon those who had the privilege of attending their original release.

We scan the centuries and we scan the light of chelas. We scan those who would be chelas but say they cannot. We look for will. We look for the momentum of the will to be. We look for those who have the courage to fling themselves into the majesty of overcoming, into the way of life victorious. We look for those who understand the light of service as the perpetual motion of the light-bearers. We look for those whose heads are not cast down, but who look into the skies to see the stars and to see in the stars the hope of life and life everlasting.

—El Morya

Contents

Welcome, Keepers of the Flame!

It is to the Order of Malta that I dedicate this seminar in The Greater Way of Freedom. Let those whose hearts burn with a desire to be free and to engender freedom in every part of life, in every facet of the consciousness of man, assemble in the capital of capitals, in the city of cities, in the nation of nations. Let them assemble while they are yet free to assemble. Let them come and worship while they are yet free to worship. Let them speak the word of the Elohim while they are yet free to speak. Let them publish abroad the truth of soul freedom while they are yet free to publish the truth.

Freedom is on the march, and the forces of freedom are marching into the capitals of the nations to enshrine the flame of freedom. High in the upper atmosphere they form the cross of Malta, and their banner is the banner of soul freedom for the Aquarian age. See their purple fires and their garments flowing—blowing in the breezes of the Holy Spirit! See the amethyst heart they wear in honor of the Cosmic Virgin! See her mantle they wear! I am come to Washington to deliver the nations in the hour of the crucifixion of the Mother that the Manchild might come forth in every heart and mind and soul as the Christ consciousness within all.

I am Saint Germain! I call the sons and daughters of liberty to defend liberty as the jewel of cosmic consciousness ensconced in the lotus flower of the heart. I come to welcome you to my focus of living flame. I come to dedicate the Rakoczy Mansion in America—the gift of Keepers of the Flame who have sealed their vows in word, in action, in manifest devotion to the greater cause of freedom.

In love and in gratitude you have called, and I have answered.

I AM

Saint Germain

I come on The Greater Way of Freedom.
Welcome!

Dedication of the Rakoczy Mansion
by Saint Germain

Lo, I AM come! Lo, I AM with you! In the light of freedom I come to dedicate this house a house of light. Let all who enter here salute the light of the I AM Presence and salute the Spirit of Freedom! I AM the invincible flame of God-protection of this house, this light, and this freedom. I place my mantle upon you who serve and you who come and you who are the instrument of the flow of my spoken Word.

I come to enshrine the light of victory for the turning of the cycle of the year. I come to inaugurate the era of the turning of the tide. While all the world of darkness tumbles over the tumbling of the dark spirits and their mumblings, the light of freedom is raised up as a star of new hope arcing with the focuses of the Great White Brotherhood throughout Terra and throughout the etheric plane.

Let it be known, then, that this house is the open door in this city to octaves of light, to contact with the etheric retreats of the Great White Brotherhood, to contact with the ascended masters. And thus Opportunity adds her flame to my own. Let it be the open portal to the unity of twin flames serving on earth as in heaven for the victory of the light.

So close is the darkness of World Communism, of all that would tear down the light of freedom! So close is the assailing of the Christ flame! But I tell you, God is closer! In the prison cell, in the dark night, God is closer! God is the invincible flame of victory that will consume on contact all that rages against the Mother within you.

Now I will give you a secret of alchemy. When you feel the momentums of opposition, the weight of oppression and depression, of the density of the mass consciousness, when you feel the irritation of the fallen ones who come unseen with their barbs of energy to disturb your

Note: "Rakoczy Mansion" is the name of the Summit International Teaching Center located at 4715 Sixteenth Street NW, Washington, D.C. This focus was purchased by Keepers of the Flame for the master Saint Germain in 1975. Following the two-day seminar "The Greater Way of Freedom," devotees of the master assembled at the center for the master's dedicatory address.

peace in the day and in the night, know that the flow of your attention upon me, Saint Germain, upon the ascended masters, and upon the I AM Presence is the light over which the fire of freedom flows.

This flow of energy will give you the indomitable will to conquer the fiery flow of destiny to be! It will give you the light of the ages to anchor the light of the flame of the Mother. And you will feel transmutation's fires pouring through you, pouring through you to consume the cause and core of that energy which rages beneath your feet and all around you, threatening, as the rattling of sabers, to swallow up the light and the fire of a cosmic destiny.

I AM Saint Germain! I enshrine freedom in this focus. I enshrine freedom in your hearts. Guard the flame! Guard the organization which surrounds the flame, guard the light in the window of the lighthouse, and guard the cube of the Church Universal and Triumphant. Guard the Manchild within you! Guard the Child becoming the master of life. Guard the Mother whose presence is essential to the victory, and guard all of the children of the Mother throughout the world who would touch the hem of the garment of Omega that she wears.

In the name of the Christ and in the name of the living flame, I salute you, one and all; and I place my mantle as a swaddling garment around this focus. Let it be for the victory of light in America and in the world! And now let us see what the chelas of Morya and Saint Germain will do as hand in hand they step right through the veil of maya into the octaves of light.

I AM with you! I AM with you all the way in your flight. Even as I took the Mother and Child out of the danger of Herod into the land of Egypt, so I take you into that place prepared—a point of light, a point of contact, a point of solace and of surcease from the world's illusions. I take you by the hand. I AM your Joseph and your Saint Germain. I AM the guardian of your flame. I AM the protector of all that shall come to pass as the fulfillment of life and light in America.

Pax vobiscum.

The Statue of the Goddess of Freedom

Armed Freedom, a statue depicting the Goddess of Freedom, crowns the dome of the United States Capitol. The statue, which has come to be known as the Statue of Freedom, portrays the goddess dressed in flowing robes, her right hand upon a sheathed sword, her left hand holding a wreath and a shield. Her head is covered by a helmet encircled with stars and surmounted by a crest composed of an eagle's head and feathers.

Few details are available about the inception of this remarkable work of American art. The artist, Thomas Crawford, sometime between 1855 and 1856 received "an invitation" from Captain Montgomery Meigs, chief engineer of the Capitol, to design the statue. Crawford, one of the foremost American sculptors of his time, had already been commissioned by Meigs to design other works in the Capitol, the most notable of which is the pediment in the Senate wing, which portrays the emergence of a great civilization in America triumphant over a barbaric way of life. In 1855 Crawford was at work on the doors for the entrance to the House and the Senate wings of the Capitol; but before the doors were completed, the artist had begun sketching an "Armed Freedom" at the invitation of Meigs. His sketch eventually resulted in the 19-foot bronze figure that stands upon the Capitol dome.

Though the particular impetus of inspiration for *Armed Freedom* is not known, Crawford, in general, was a highly inspired artist. He is reported to have kept a room above his studio full of small clay sketches and sculptural ideas that came to him while he was working on larger projects. "The flow of his ideas was of such force and insistence that he often had to stop work on his monuments to dash off these little models. Sculptural ideas seemed 'to rise spontaneously and intuitively at Crawford's bidding. He hit off his marble epics as a poet would turn a graceful stanza,'" wrote historian Albert G. Gardner. And he himself wrote, "I regret that I have not a hundred hands to keep pace with the workings of my mind."

His inspiration saw him through at least two bouts with an eye tumor, which eventually led to his death in 1857, just shortly after he completed the model of *Armed Freedom*. He is said to have been in "severe agony" during the final months of his work. The statue was cast between 1860 and 1863 by Clark Mills, another American artist, in a foundry just three miles from the Capitol. Though the Civil War had broken out in 1861, President Lincoln is known to have insisted that work on the Capitol dome—to him a symbol of national solidarity—continue.

Finally, on December 2, 1863, *Armed Freedom* was enshrined atop the Capitol dome. The President watched as the last section of the statue was raised into place, and the event was heralded by a 35-gun salute.

On November 23, 1975, Saint Germain placed the flame of freedom in the heart of this statue. He said: "I select the monument, the focal point for the enshrining of freedom; and I place that focus of freedom in the heart of America, in the very heart chakra of the Goddess of Freedom reigning over the Capitol building of the United States. And there the heart chakra of the Divine Mother shall broadcast the fires of freedom from the crystal of the heart, from the twelve fiery focal points of the mandala of her crystal. So shall freedom from the twelve hierarchies of the sun go forth and beam that arc of light to the heart of the Statue of Liberty."

Armed Freedom

The Prophecy of the Soul of America
by Elizabeth Clare Prophet

Prophecy is the statement of the servants of God, cosmic beings known as the Lords of Individuality, given to their messengers or prophets embodied in the worlds of time and space. It is a statement of opportunity outlining what the people of a given planet, nation, race, or culture have the option, within a certain frame and forcefield of time and space, of choosing to do and to become in God.

Prophecy is not a psychic prediction; it is not an astrological forecast; it is not the product of divination or of crystal-ball gazing. Prophecy is a statement of what the future can be, given mankind's implementation of free will in the past and in the present. Prophecy is written from the original blueprint of men and nations progressed from the alteration of that blueprint by free will that has resulted in the karma and the dharma of men and nations.

Prophecies are fulfilled by the free will of the people whose actions, guided by the hand of Providence and graced by the Holy Spirit, may fulfill the blueprint of an epoch within the larger mandala of an age. Prophecies can fail when people choose to go against the will of God, thereby aborting his plan. They can also fail, as in the case of Jonah, when people repent of their evil ways and thereby forestall dire calamity, cataclysm, epidemic, or economic adversity.

Prophecy is the means used by the Elohim to define mankind's current opportunity to master the self and thereby master time and space. Prophecy is a statement of opportunity for initiation to a planet and a people. Prophecy is a warning given to mankind when they have gotten out of alignment with the inner law of being—a warning of consequences if and when they fail to respond to the discipline of the flame within. Those who hear the certain word of prophecy and run with it are the forerunners of the new dispensation and the new age.

As we celebrate America's Bicentennial, we bow before the Lord of the Universe whose hand has guided the destiny of this nation from its inception. The Declaration of Independence made by the people who laid the foundation of America the free, the abundant, the beautiful, was the initiation of a spiral of cosmic consciousness that would be fulfilled only when the generations who were to call themselves Americans would one day declare their independence from the tyranny of the not-self and from the bondage of every form of selfishness and ego-centered existence.

The two-hundred-year celebration of the Declaration of Independence marks a moment when we the people who would preserve this nation must pause to study the past and the present in order to determine the course of the future. The Lord God is the Prophet of our destiny. Let us listen to his certain word and respond with our own prophecy for the fulfillment of the divine mandate.

The following Prophecy of America was delivered to me by the Lords of Individuality. May it serve every American to more clearly define his own individualization of the God flame and thereby contribute to the Spirit of oneness and to the fulfillment of the karma and the dharma of America—fifty states united in the one flame of freedom given to us to give to the nations and peoples of the earth.

The Prophecy of America is implemented by and for the will of the people through the twelve hierarchies of the sun who serve the Lord God to anchor the twelve aspects of God consciousness in the galaxies, systems of worlds, and in the planets and their evolutions. From the God Star Sirius, seat of God-government in our galaxy, the twelve Solar Lords, through the Four and Twenty Elders, have sealed the destiny of earth as freedom's star and of America as the place prepared for the realization of the Christ consciousness of freedom.

Certain of these twelve hierarchies were selected by Alpha and Omega in the Great Central Sun to guide the souls whose evolution qualified them to come to Terra, to America, to the place in the wilderness, the land that would be the heart of freedom to the earth. The hierarchy of Aquarius was selected to give to the soul of America the initiations in the flame of freedom—initiations of alchemy that the soul might realize the oneness of the flame in the creativity that marks the true genius of the legions of Aquarius.

Coming into the new age, then, directed by Aquarius, the soul of America must also come of age. Her genius rising in a spiral, ever pushing the limits of freedom to larger dimensions of consciousness, the soul of America is being prepared to define that freedom which is the ultimate discipline of the self according to the will of God. When the soul of America gains self-mastery in the flame of Aquarius, it will expand true freedom to every nation with a fervor that will not be quenched and the golden age that is to be on Terra will be realized as the age of Aquarius.

To the hierarchy of Libra was assigned the duty of tutoring the people of America in the establishment of God-government and in the balance of the masculine and feminine rays as well as of the mental and feeling bodies. In the Constitution are set forth those laws which establish a rule of love in the freedom of the Holy Spirit which is the balance of the Father-Mother God in Libra. Americans must take the reins of authority from those who have usurped them and become the masters of self-rule in a representative form of government. This they will do in response to the tutoring of their souls in the wisdom of the Mother.

To the hierarchy of Cancer was assigned the task of teaching the American people to realize their full God-potential in the consciousness of the Divine Mother. Our dealings with one another and with other nations are governed by the hierarchies of Cancer and Libra, showing the way of the Mother and the Holy Spirit as the way of freedom. America is to present to the world the archetype of the Divine Manchild—the Christ consciousness—that must be born in every nation. America is the child of *innocence* that must come to full maturity ere it realizes through its *inner sense* the sacred mystery of its fiery destiny.

Thus it is the hand of the Divine Mother, symbolized in the statue of the Goddess of Liberty, that will be extended as the hand of comfort, enlightenment, peace, and plenty when, through meditation within and action without, Americans realize the true feminine potential of both men and women. Liberty is the spirit of the Divine Mother in America. In her left hand she holds the book of the law, her gift to a free people, theirs to give to all people. The law is the sacred teaching for the ruling of the cities and the nations by those who will first rule the spirit.

The torch which the Divine Mother carries in her right hand is a torch of liberty—a liberty that is realized in self-mastery through disciplined love and a wisdom founded on obedience to the will of God. The torch of liberty is the torch of the aspirations of the souls of the children of the Mother toward the enlightenment of the Christ and the Buddha. Thus from her place prepared in the wilderness land, the Divine Mother will direct her children throughout the world to the path of the Christ and the Buddha.

The victorious sense is a part of the soul destiny of America bestowed by the hierarchy of Sagittarius, who teaches the members of the I AM race how to "be fruitful and multiply and replenish the earth and subdue it" in the victorious light of freedom. It is by the flame of victory that the American people will take dominion over the planes of Matter, leading the world in the conquest of time and space, solving the problems of energy, ecology, and the flow of the resources of the abundant life.

The twelve hierarchies of the sun teach us that the threefold flame is the key to the realization of America's fiery destiny. The threefold flame of power, wisdom, and love that is the spark of divinity in every son and daughter of God is the flame of the Christ and the Buddha. It is the balance of the Trinity in manifestation, burning as a sacred fire on the altar of every heart. This flame is the individuality of the sons and daughters of God. When the flame is balanced in outer manifestation within the individual and in the historical evolution of any nation, then the citizens and the nation forming a unit in the mandala of hierarchy can make their unique contribution to the world.

The first hundred years of America's history was based on the blue ray of power implemented in the setting-forth of our government, our laws, and the pioneer expansion under the aegis of *God the Father*. The second hundred years was based on the development of the yellow ray of wisdom in the stimulus of education and culture under the aegis of *God the Son* in Christed sons and daughters. The third hundred years will be the development of the pink ray of love under *God the Holy Spirit*, who will unite the people in love. This will be an opportunity for the culmination of science and religion as the two pillars in the temple of the people and for the completion of the trinity of the threefold flame of liberty which will burn on the altar of the temple.

The opportunity for America in the next century is for her people to balance the flame of the Christ within themselves and thereby come into the understanding of the white-fire core of the threefold flame—the purity of *God the Mother* who is the foundation of life in Matter. Therefore, the next hundred years will be the rounding-out of the sense of love through the Holy Spirit and the balancing of the threefold flame of Father, Son, and Holy Spirit in and as the action of the Mother in Matter. This can be done only as the people willingly, wisely, and lovingly accept the initiations of Christ and Buddha given by the Divine Mother.

The Bicentennial birthday celebration of America marks the opening of the period when the people of the United States, recognizing their identity as the true Israelites, as sons and daughters of God, and as children of the Mother, can and shall assert their responsibility in establishing God-government—of the people, by the people, and for the people—that soul freedom shall not perish from the earth. In taking up the torch of the founding fathers who established the thirteen colonies on the basis of the mandala of the original thirteen—Christ and his disciples—the people of America will undergo the initiations of the sacred fire that will lead them on the same path that Christ and Buddha walked. And though the agony of the crucifixion be at hand, the dawn of the resurrection will reveal the hope of life eternal to all evolutions on Terra.

The pattern of the thirteen—the pattern of initiation for Christhood—was established by the Lord when he was in Jerusalem. It will be transferred to America as the New Jerusalem when the people realize their responsibility to take their thirty-three initiations in the Christ consciousness under the twelve hierarchies of the sun. Only by submitting to the tests of the sacred fire will they reestablish the perfect union of God and man begun in Spirit, materialized in the culture of the Mother and her children, there to be reconfirmed in the flame of the Holy Spirit.

Unless unity is established in America through the establishment of self-identity first within the individual, then within the community, and then within the nation, she will not realize the victory of the flame of oneness which is the fusion in the Christ of the light of the twelve hierarchies reflected through the twelve tribes of Israel.

It is the good fortune of America to have etched in the blueprint of her fiery destiny the responsibility of the raising-up of the feminine ray. This includes the mastery of the planes of Matter through science and religion, the restoration of the freedom of woman, which she must earn through obedience to the inner laws which govern her being, through the mastery of the flow of the energies of air, fire, water, and earth, and through the raising of the fires of the kundalini—the Mother flow whose origin is at the base of the spine—which rises to contact the light of the Christ in the heart and of God the Father in the crown chakra.

As America accords to woman the reward of her self-mastery, restoring the woman liberated by enlightenment to her proper position as mother, teacher, visionary, and leader, America will find her true place among the nations. A culture and a civilization can rise no higher than the level which that culture and civilization accords to woman. Only through accepting the initiations of the Mother flame can the women of America liberate themselves and their children, their husbands, brothers, fathers, and companions in life.

As man gives to woman the freedom to express her creativity according to cosmic law, he opens the door to his own liberation from the bondage of every form of ego-attachment. America is the open door to freedom which no man can shut. Only woman can shut the door by her failure to respond to her ability to take dominion over the forces that govern her destiny.

America is destined to lead the way in the education of the child, the elevation of the child's consciousness to the place of reverence in life, to the training of children in the community of the Holy Spirit which we share with all nations, and in the initiations of Christ and Buddha. America must lead the world in the path of enlightenment as her institutions of learning are brought into balance, placing equal emphasis on the flames of Spirit and Matter.

As we have laid the foundation of the conquest of Matter and of time and space according to the Judeo-Christian tradition of the law of the Father and the light of the Son, so we must lay the foundation of education based on a spiritualization of Matter according to the traditions of the love of the Mother and the discipline of the Holy Spirit.

Many souls of great light are destined to be born in 1976, and our mentors of the Spirit have requested on at least three occasions that the devotees of freedom pray for their safe passageway through the portals of birth. The Lords of Karma welcome petitions through parents who would sponsor these souls who are to inaugurate a new cycle in America's destiny. This is the year of the dedication of the family as a holy family, as life giving and receiving life, as the love of twin flames "as above, so below" ushering in the souls of the new age for the deliverance of a planet and a people.

The birthday cycle of America is an opportunity for the healing of the economy and the government at all levels. It is an auspicious moment for the invocation of the all-seeing eye of God as the capstone on the pyramid that is the symbol of the new order of the ages.

Nineteen seventy-six marks the year of the return of the masters of the Far East, of members of the Great White Brotherhood to the West, to establish their teaching and the path of soul liberation. The ascended masters will come to the forefront of the nation in the final twenty-five years of the century which mark the first quarter of the new birthday cycle.

The people's devotion to the Elohim as the seven spirits of creation will give balance to the mental and feeling bodies, to the interplay of energies between mind and heart, body and soul. The influx of light from the Great Central Sun coursing through the four lower bodies of the earth and her evolutions puts ever-increasing strain on the vehicles of consciousness. Therefore, correct meditation according to the teachings of the masters of the Great White Brotherhood will be essential to the maintenance of mental, emotional, and physical health.

The science of the spoken Word is the instrument which the masters who guide the destiny of America have given to the people they have chosen to carry the torch of freedom to the world. If the American people will use that science, together with correct techniques of meditation, become active in government, assume responsibility in the community, and sustain the flame of the Holy Spirit as the basis of love between man and woman, between parents and children, they will pass through the fiery trials, the temptations, and the testings that will be for the strengthening, the ennobling, and the elevation of a mighty people—a people destined to be conquerors of the self that they might be the servants of all.

It is up to the American people to enlarge the borders of cosmic consciousness, beginning with the home and widening to include the cities that are intended to be citadels of God consciousness, the plains and the mountains that are designed to be open spaces for the purifying action of the Holy Spirit. As the God-dominion of the soul is established through self-discipline, so the borders of cosmic consciousness will expand in concentric rings to include the entire earth, that all nations might find the same canopy of grace, bounty, and joy that is the flame of America.

America is moving forward into the vastness of cosmic consciousness. This movement, typified by the prophetic appearance of the Comet Kohoutek, will precipitate the confrontation of every soul with the Woman in the Apocalypse and her Divine Manchild. This confrontation will produce either calamity, chaos, confusion, disease and death, or the resurrection of the nations and the peoples of the earth into a golden-age civilization through a higher level of self-awareness and self-esteem.

It is up to sons and daughters of God who know who they are and who are known by Love to teach the children of the Mother that the path of initiation is the path to attainment. Truly the response over the next century of those to whom the responsibility has been given will tell the destiny and the future not only of the people of America, but of the entire human race.

The test of the love ray is always more difficult than the test of the will and the wisdom. What America does with the great influx of love which will descend from the heart of the Elohim on July 4, 1976, will determine what happens in the coming decades and by the year 2001—a significant date in the prophecy of the Great Pyramid. What happens in the next twenty-five years will determine the course of the remainder of the third hundred years of our nation's birth, and this in turn will determine the fate of civilization on earth.

Truly free will is the key to the fulfillment of prophecy. As John F. Kennedy said, "On earth God's work must truly be our own." O America, let us pray that by his grace we shall make the right choices for freedom, that by his Spirit we shall put down every form of tyranny that assails the mind of man, that by the Mother and the Son we shall restore purity, nobility, and reverence for life in our children, in our youth, and in the soul that is America.

I

The Fiery Destiny of America
by the Spirit of Freedom
in the Fourteen Ascended Masters
Who Govern the Destiny of America

Let the fires of freedom roll from the heart of America, from the heart of the Great Central Sun! Let the fires of freedom roll!

I AM in the Spirit of the Fourteen Ascended Masters who come forth from the Royal Teton Retreat to anchor the electrodes of the initiations of the fourteen that America might fulfill her destiny in the flame of the Mother and in the flame of the Christed one. I AM the arc of light arcing the star of invincible Christ-awareness from the focus in the Royal Teton to your own heart flame.

I come in the name of the law! I come in the name of liberty! And I come for the fulfillment of the soul of a nation, the soul of a people, and the soul of a planet. By the fiery action of the star—fourteen points of light quickening as the Alpha-to-the-Omega within you—draw forth the consciousness of overcoming, of clear seeing, of the action of the seven rays in the white-fire core for the release of the secret rays of the Mother.

America is in the stage of the quickening and in the age of the becoming of the fullness of a destiny held in the heart of the Elohim, held in the heart of Saint Germain,

held in the heart of us who have held this fiery destiny as
the seed atom of light. And so in the atom is the blueprint
of life and in the atom is the quickening.

There are some who have been called from near and
from far to be in America in this hour. These are the lively
stones whose fiery consciousness reflects the blueprint of
the victory.[1] And in the fiery electrodes of the heart, these
ones are called as sons and daughters of God who have
incarnated from etheric cities of light to be the fulfillment
of the plan of freedom in this age.

There are some who have come because they have
sensed the calling, the homing of the Elohim; and they are
also in America waiting for the appearance of the star and
the fixing of the star in the embodied ones chosen as the
chosen of God to be the reality of the flame. These are the
children of the sun who await the coming of the Christ in
the second coming of that flame.

There are others waiting in the sidelines because they
sense, as it were, the marching of the angels. And there are
those who are always there to watch the parade. These are
the ones who have not the commitment of the flame—
neither the responsibility of the sons and daughters of God
or the quickening of the lively stones. But they are the
ones who watch; hence they are called the watchers. And
they watch while the light-bearers garner the light for the
victory. They would seize the light in the hour of the
victory. I say: They shall not! They shall not pass! They
shall not seize the light of the children of the Mother in
the day of overcoming!

And so the angels come; they come to wrap the
children in the swaddling garment of light. This is the
swaddling garment that is composed of the banner of
Maitreya and of the World Mother. The World Mother
takes her banner and wraps in it the Divine Manchild and
seals the light becoming light within the hearts of the
people by her all-enfolding love. And the angels of the
Divine Mother come! They are approaching this system of

worlds. They come from afar. They come in answer to the calls made unto Omega by the children of the sun.

Omega sends her legions of the flame. Omega sends legions for the binding of the fallen ones—the spectators of life who sit in the sidelines. And they eat their popcorn, watching the great battle of Armageddon and the notable day of the Lord![2] Thus those who have failed to choose to be active as workers in the works of righteousness—they are sealed. For the angels of the Mother know whereof they come; and they know the whys of existence, and they understand the coming of the light, and they understand the pressures upon the children of the light. And they come to support the sons and daughters of God who have the name "I AM THAT I AM"[3] written within their hearts as the mantra of the flame that consumes the mark of the beast and those who carry that mark.[4]

I AM come in the Spirit of the Elohim for the fulfillment of the cycles of America's victory. This is the land prepared to receive the Christed ones, that they might mature in the Christ flame that they might raise up the light of the Mother and carry it afar—from nation to nation—lighting the star of divinity. Thus the Goddess of Liberty holds high her torch.

And in this hour, the arcing of attainment is the weaving of the mandala as the crocheting of the Mother, the weaving of the mandala spanning a world enveloped in the consciousness of "I AM America's victory!"

The victory of America is not the victory of a nation. It is the victory of the twelve hierarchies of the sun in the twelve tribes of Israel[5] who have come forth from every nation to dip into the flame, who shall return to every nation to ignite the flame, who shall be unto all people the carriers of the fires of freedom.

Let the runners in the race, then, hear the cry of the Fourteen Ascended Masters! Ours is a cry for freedom throughout the land of Terra! Ours is a cry for the Divine Mother! Ours is a cry of liberation for the souls of humanity! Let the fires of freedom roll from the heart of the Royal Teton!

Souls of humanity, be quickened by the fires! For we send forth the unmistakable light, the invincible light—the light of victory. And it is a magnet in the sky that comes now in the fulfillment of the hierarchies of victory who stand in the flame of Sagittarius, giving birth to the light of victory presaging the light of the Divine Manchild and the Spirit of the Christ Mass. In the flame of victory is the victory of the Mother and her children! In the flame of victory is the fulfillment of the light of souls, of the light of every nation.

The action which is taking place as I am speaking is the drawing of elements of consciousness as above so below, as above so below, as above so below. Elements of the human consciousness are cycling into the flame of the Divine Mother as that flame is being raised—raised on high as the focus of that star, the star of victory in the sky. This is the moment of the raising of the energies of the life of the Mother. This is the moment of the raising of her banner, and legions of angels raise high that banner in the sign of the victory of the Mother flame.

It is a banner which will blow in the breeze with the flag of every nation. It is a banner which blows in the breeze with the banner of Maitreya. Thus the World Teachers consecrate the banner of the Great Initiator, Maitreya, and the banner of the Cosmic Virgin. And these shall be in the place in every nation where the flag of that nation is raised on high in tribute to the Christ consciousness of that nation and to the fulfillment of the karma and the dharma of that nation.

Wherever you see then the flags of the nations—Old Glory and each and every flag that symbolizes the spirit of a people throughout the earth—know that the Fourteen Ascended Masters who govern the destiny of this nation and of the golden-age cultures of Terra have also raised high the banner of Maitreya and the banner of the Mother.

Thus is the hour of the victory proclaimed and the trinity of consciousness for the fulfillment of the fiery destiny of every living soul and of every nation.

This is the goal and this is the thrust of our victory for the year 1976. We begin in the capital of the United States of America; and we go from nation to nation, preparing the way for the coming of Saint Germain, who is to enshrine the flame of freedom in every nation upon earth. Let this seminar, then, be consecrated by the twin flames of Alpha and Omega, who sponsor the victory of your souls.

This is the hour of the holding of the hands high over America and over all of the nations—the hands of mighty Victory, the hands of Maitreya and of the Great Divine Director. This is the moment of the coming of cosmic beings who are standing by Saint Germain, the Lord of the Seventh Ray, the God of Freedom to the earth. Cosmic beings sent by cosmic councils come in this hour of the turning of the cycles of hierarchy to stand with the Master of Freedom, to enshrine freedom, and to deliver America and every nation unto the arms of the Divine Mother and the everlasting Christ.

Souls of God-free beings, souls of chelas, souls of all life, hear the pealing of the liberty bell! Hear the bell of freedom that proclaims the awakening of the heart of a nation! Hear now the declaration of independence of souls throughout a planetary body. Hear then! For the light of far-off worlds is come and there is a saturation of Terra by the lords of flame from Venus, the holy Kumaras, who endow life and consciousness with increments of the mind of God by the crystal of the mind of God. They are also radiating to Terra the flame of mighty Victory, the flame of lady master Venus.

We who stand in the Royal Teton holding the points of light of the fourteen initiations of the sons and daughters of God in the cosmic cross of white fire bow before the Lord of Flame, the hierarch of Venus, Sanat

Kumara. This is a moment of the initiation of the cycles of victory as the children of the One submit to the initiations of Maitreya and fulfill them in the teaching of the World Mother. Let all who love life, let all who live for freedom, respond to the call of the Great White Brotherhood! Let them respond from near and from far!

And I proclaim this hour the dispensation of Saint Germain that every living soul upon earth who is dedicated to the cause of the Great White Brotherhood, within or without, consciously aware or not, shall receive the teaching of the Mother, the teaching of the law that is given forth at Summit University. And the teachings of the Buddha, the Lord of the World, which shall come forth in the winter quarter of this university, shall be beamed directly to the souls who have made their covenant and their commitment to the flame. Thus it is the desire of Saint Germain that that word of the law from the heart of the Lord of the World, from the heart of Maitreya, and from the heart of Omega shall be anchored in those souls in every nation who are keeping the flame of life and freedom for the hierarchies of light.

We come in the flame of victory! We seal you in the light of victory! We seal you in the light of the Elohim for the victory of the year of freedom! I AM in the Spirit of Liberty. I AM in the Spirit of the Council of the Royal Teton.

II

The Karma of America
by the Goddess of Liberty

I come from the Temple of the Sun with a message of victory for the people of America and the people of the world. I come as the spokesman for the Lords of Karma. I come in the feminine ray of truth to exalt that truth of the feminine ray within you. I come to speak of karma as the law of cause and effect and karma as the destiny not only of America, but of every nation upon earth.

You have heard of individual influence within the self and within the family and within the community at large. I say that the influence which the individual can exercise and which the individual nation can exert rests squarely on the proposition of karma. Where you are in consciousness rests upon karma. Many among you have very good karma; karma then becomes your opportunity to fulfill your divine plan. And none of you are without those negative aspects of karma that have brought your souls into incarnation on Terra once again to try again to fulfill the law of an inner destiny which God has willed and you have affirmed.

I AM the Goddess of Liberty. I have stood before each and every one of you as you have passed before the Lords of Karma prior to taking incarnation in this life. Now I am activating the memory in your soul of this experience of speaking with me. Look into the face with your inner eye—my own face and that face focused in the Statue of Liberty. Recall now this gaze of the one who represented the Divine Mother to you. Recall the admonishment of your soul and your vow made to me in person to go forth, to carry that torch of liberty, to give rebirth to the Christ flame and the Christ consciousness.

You are here in America—some by birth and some by the destiny of your karma. You find yourself in this place in time and space because I made a commitment to you in the hour of your birth that you would come to know the teachings of the ascended masters, that you would meet those lifestreams who could impart to you the knowledge of the law and the knowledge of your vow. I promised you that you would meet my representative of the Mother flame.

Why did I make this promise? Because each and every one of you who is seated here tonight expressed the concern to me, as the Mother flame, that you would forget the knowledge of the sacred fire, the law of your karma, and your promise to keep the flame of life; and you implored me to promise you that you would have the opportunity to know the law.

Therefore, I have fulfilled this night my vow to many of you and you are here. And so I also expect, as you expected of me, that you will fulfill your inner vow to the Lords of Karma and to Saint Germain to make a more than ordinary effort in this life to balance your karma and to make yourself available for the fulfillment of America's destiny, to take the flame of the Mother and the Christed ones and to expand that flame into the world dominion of the Christ consciousness.

Well, we have come into a time, into an age, when it is imperative that those who have made their vows to keep the flame do so. Therefore I proclaim again! Liberty proclaims within you the law of your inner being and the understanding that now is the time and the space for the light of your own God Presence to shine within you. Now is the time to forsake the careless expense and waste of God's energies of the natural resources of the Spirit—the energy that flows ceaselessly.

Now is the time to realize that your Christ Self is able to reverse the tide of darkness on Terra, that in that flame is the power, the wisdom of God to become the allness of God in manifestation. Now is the time to prove the law of the avatars. Now is the time to make yourself a part of the mainstream of the karmic destiny of America, for her destiny is to be the place where the Woman clothed with the Sun and with a crown of twelve stars rises to deliver the mandate of the Christ consciousness and to give birth to that Christ Child.[1] This is the Mother within you.

I have with me, then, the assurance of Portia of opportunity sealed and the dispensation of our board to give opportunity to this group of devotees for a more than ordinary release of the fires of the Mother within you that your soul might be nourished by the Mother's love. For you yourself have earned this dispensation; you have given service to that Mother flame. Sometime, somewhere, your devotion and your service has been sealed. And so we capitalize on good karma this night to allow us to enter into the forcefield of your world, to unlock the fires of the Mother, and to seal the raising of those fires for a manifestation of the God consciousness within you—a sealing of the light of the heart, that you might understand and become the Christ.

It is America's destiny to reveal the culture of the Mother to the world. And the hierarchies of Aries and Libra, fulfilling the light of the heart chakra, come to the aid of those who have heard the call and felt the flame throughout Terra, throughout the four planes of Mater. The hierarchies of the sun come forth and their proclamation is this: That it is by the fires of the Holy Spirit and the all-consuming energy of your own I AM Presence that you will bring into manifestation the fulfillment of this fiery destiny.

Now therefore, receive the assignment of the Lords of Karma, that assignment being to surrender a portion of misqualified energy into the flame that it might be transmuted, that you might have returned to you God's energy purified to work the works of God on earth. The assignment from the Lords of Karma is to give the mantras and the invocations to the violet flame for the freeing of this nation, for the reestablishment of spirals of victory to move forward during this period of the Dark Cycle and to establish the initiation of another one-hundred-year cycle wherein the initiations of Maitreya can be given, wherein the teachings of the Mother can be proclaimed and the Mother's children can come into the fountain of living flame and have their chakras nourished, their souls and hearts and minds nourished by the fires of living love, of immortal truth.

The flame of the Mother burns and expands. The heart of the Divine Mother calls the children of the One into the AUM, and that calling to the home is the calling of consciousness back to the awareness of reality.

It is the karmic destiny of America to experiment in God-government, to experiment with the divine documents of liberty. It is the destiny of America to establish golden-age education. And in the education that is the unfoldment of the heart chakra, it is the destiny for the little children to rise up with that God-dominion and that mastery of the quadrants of Mater whereby they can teach to all nations the way of overcoming on the path of initiation under the Christ and the Buddha and the inner law written in the inward parts.[2]

So it is the destiny of America to fulfill the culture as science—a science that liberates souls from drudgery and the toiling that became the karma of those who were expelled from the God consciousness of Eden. And this science is the technology of the Divine Mother. It must not be misused or abused. It must become, with religion, the pillar in the temple of being, so that by the binding of the individual to God as Father in religion and the binding of the individual to Mother in Mater in science, the aspects twofold of Spirit and Matter may be fulfilled within the individual.

The culture of the Mother is not to be despised. The championing of the individual God flame ought not to be misused through those who take advantage by greed of the system of capitalism and free enterprise. These are to be bound by the action of the sacred fire of the Lords of Karma; for those who misuse the Spirit of the individuality of the God flame are perverting the flow of abundance, the flow of the supply of God, into the hands of the children of God.

Let this nation, then, be restored to the divine economy and the divine principles of government. Let the essence of these principles be drawn from the Source, the one Source of the I AM THAT I AM, the true lawgiver of each individual God flame. Let there be a restoration, a regeneration, a rejuvenation, and a resurrection of life in the four lower bodies of those who have chosen to be a free people! And let this choosing be transferred to every nation. Let the example be set and let it be transferred!

I speak to all who love freedom in every nation on earth: Fulfill the light of your karmic destiny! Work to give forth the culture of the Mother in your nation! Whether it be Mother Russia or Mother India or Mother China or Mother America, let it be that the souls of the children of the One Flame respond to the call of the Mother in their own tongue, in their own culture.

And let their cultures be purified by the flow of the flaming ones—sons and daughters of God ascended, cosmic beings who gather at Terra at the portals of consciousness to accelerate God consciousness, to exalt those who would be exalted in the God flame, to bring to pass the saying that is written, "Death is swallowed up in victory."[3] So let that culture of death which is not a culture be swallowed up in the victory of life, and let life flow from the heart of the Mother to her children. Let the life that is God be the fulfillment of the fiery destiny of the individual unto the nation, unto the planet, unto souls and evolutions who must come forth to fulfill their divine plan on earth.

And this brings me to the question of population control. I am very concerned with the control of the incarnation of lifewaves on Terra, for we who are the Lords of Karma plan the incarnation of souls who will contribute to the overall pattern of perfectionment on earth. We are the ones who pass on souls who apply for incarnation. Out of every one who applies, there are two who remain, who must be denied entrée into the portals of birth. Out of everyone whose incarnation is granted, there are percentages who never reach incarnation because of the current trends toward birth control through the abortion of life.

And then there is that planning by those who advocate zero population growth, and there is the indoctrination in the mass consciousness against giving birth to children in this age. And therefore, those very precious and important lifestreams whom we have assigned to Terra are denied entrance into Terra by the free will of mothers and fathers who have taken the vow to give birth to souls but who have accepted the brainwashing of the mass consciousness.

I am a mother conscious of the Mother flame in cosmic dimensions and I am very conscious of the gaps in the evolutionary chain of hierarchy now occurring on Terra. I am concerned with coming decades and the absence of those lifestreams who have been denied opportunity to live, to move, to breathe, to overcome, to attain God-mastery on Terra.

What will you do in twenty-five years when the scientists and the great avatars and those who espouse mankind's freedom, those who are returning to liberate the masses, are not there because you have denied them life? What will you do when the ages turn, when there are wars and rumors of wars and pestilence and plague and cataclysm taking the life of many, when the dearth of population comes and there is not the replacement for those souls whose karma will take them from the screen of life? What will you do, O mankind who have made yourselves prey—fodder—for the manipulators? You have believed the lie; and as it is written, your condemnation is just, because you will have made your own karma.[4] As you say, you make your bed and you lie in it.

This is the story of karma; karma is the exercise of free will. I ask you now, have you exercised free will or have you been manipulated? You do not exercise free will until you know both sides of the story. Did you know this side of the story before I spoke to you? Did you know that there are thousands of Christed ones awaiting incarnation? You have been told of their courage. You have heard that they come, they are aborted, and they volunteer again, knowing that they may pass through that trauma of dying in their mother's wombs. Yet they volunteer again because they are determined to set life free!

They are far more determined than many of mankind embodied to liberate the masses; for they see above and beyond the manipulation of the death cult; and therefore they see your souls crying out, pleading with the Lords of Karma for help, for intercession. They behold the prayers of children; they behold the praying of babies in their mothers' wombs praying for life, praying they will come to maturation to be born in Mater—souls waiting to incarnate who are mature, advanced lifestreams not only from Terra but from other planetary bodies and even volunteers from other systems of worlds.

They have knocked on the doors of the Lords of Karma in our chambers in the Royal Teton Retreat. They have pleaded for opportunity. We have shown them what they will be up against and yet they have said: "We will go; we will try! We will work with mothers and fathers; we will find our place. We will find room in the inn on Terra." And so they come and they continue to come.

Now see what the question of abortion brings as karma to the feet of a nation! See what war brings as karma to the feet of a nation! Understand that those who kill with the sword must be killed by the sword.[5] Whether the sword is on the battlefield or in the surgeon's hand, the taking of life bears the consequence. And these consequences place a heavy karma on the people of America whose destiny it is to bring forth the Christ consciousness not only in the little children, but through the sacred fires of the heart.

As the Spirit of Christmas covers the land with the light of the I AM Presence, that Spirit of the Christ Mass comes knocking also at the door of your heart, asking that you might pray for the little ones that they might be born in this auspicious year of 1976, that they might come as the crown of rejoicing of the Goddess of Liberty in celebration of freedom and of life and of living and of the giving of self.

I tell you, precious ones, there is no greater fulfillment in all of cosmos than the fulfillment of creation— a holy maternity, a holy paternity, father and mother standing as representatives of the Father-Mother God giving birth to the Christ Child. Unless the fulfillment of creation be manifest within you, whether by giving birth to a child or by giving birth to the Christ light in lifestreams, you will not know the fulfillment of cycles.

Do you understand that the manipulators of the souls of humanity would take from them the fulfillment of the cycles of creation—would abort those cycles? Is it any wonder that we have a sick society and sick people because they are not allowed to create in the image and likeness of God, but they are told to create the ugly and the sordid and the astral and the psychic and the discordant sounds and art forms. And thus deep within the psyche, deep within the souls of mankind, there is a longing to be free to create as God creates.

O the wonder of creation! The wonder of watching before your very eyes a friend, a member of your family, being transformed in the image of the living God because you have allowed yourself to be the instrument of that flame! O the wonder of wonders to see the newborn child and the rebirth in the Spirit! You can be instruments for the magnetization of the God flame. You can be instruments for the salvation of a planet and a people.

I speak it now and I will speak it again and again; for I am delivering into your total consciousness, being, and world the promise of life and of victory through the fulfillment of your vows. I stand before you fearless in the face of the carnal mind and the mass manipulations of the carnal mind! For I know that one word spoken now in your own heart as a prayer to God to transmute that influence—to commit it to the flame—will be answered instantaneously by the edict of the Lords of Karma.

I therefore give you an opportunity, a moment of silence, to make your prayer to Almighty God; for in this cosmic moment there is opportunity of legions of angels who come to intercede and to bring to your hearts that which you invoke in the light of freedom. [Silence] The Lord Christ has said, "Ask and ye shall receive; knock and it shall be opened unto you."[6] Each and every prayer uttered in the heart is adjusted now by the wisdom of your Christ Self and by the action of the will of God; and therefore any who ask amiss will find their calls adjusted in the Christ consciousness and the answer to the call will be forthcoming.

Some of you have asked for a world and some of you have asked for the individual. Know this, children of the sun—that God is not limited, that the infinite consciousness of God can fulfill your prayer for the one or for the billions of souls with equal flow and equanimity, with equal action of the fire of freedom. Therefore I say, whatever call you have made for an individual, according to the will of God and in keeping with that will, it shall be multiplied for every lifestream on Terra.

This is my promise and the fulfillment of that promise, that you might understand each and every day of your life, that that which you call forth for all mankind will be fulfilled for all mankind. We refer to this as the maximizing of your calls. Do not limit your calls then! But realize that if you pray for one who is sick, there are millions who are sick and millions more who know not that they are sick who require healing in the mind and in the emotions and in the subconscious. Therefore, let the multiplication of the loaves and the fishes by your own Christ Self be for the feeding of the multitudes through your invocations and decrees. And do not fail to include in your decrees, "This which I call forth for myself and my family, I call forth for all mankind and all evolutions of Terra on every plane of consciousness."

So then, watch how the Divine Mother will answer your calls made in the name of the living Christ. Understand the truth that the call does compel the answer. And let me if you will by your free will release now into your forcefield the flame of faith, the flame of hope, and the flame of charity amplified by the angels of Liberty who come now to maximize in the field of your consciousness your faith in the law of God, your faith in the science of the spoken Word and the science of the aura, your faith in the teachings of the ascended masters, your hope in your own Christ Self for salvation, and the charity which is the flow of the flame giving and receiving and being the outpouring and the inflowing, the unfolding and the infolding, of the sacred fires of love descending from the Most High God.

O America, fulfill your destiny and free mankind to fulfill their destiny! Stop the slaughter of the holy innocents,[7] and give birth to the Christ children who come knocking at the doors of America because this is the place where destiny must be forged and won. Must we send them then to other nations—to China, to Russia, to India, to those places where there is not the control of life—or will you give them room? I place this question before America this night and I demand that you give answer! Either you make room for the avatars and the Christed ones or the torch will be passed and other nations who will prepare them room, who will make way for the coming of the Christ, will receive this dispensation of the avatars.

I am knocking at the door of America this night! I demand answer and I ask for the prayers of the Keepers of the Flame for the American people, for their enlightenment, for their awakening in this age. When you deny the Mother flame, you deny the Christ Child. When you deny the Christ Child, you deny your own salvation. For salvation is through each and every one of these little ones who come to be admitted to raise up a golden-age civilization which yet can be born in this nation and throughout the nations of the world.

Now let the Keepers of the Flame be solemn in their consideration. You play the role of mediator; you stand in the place of the Christ consciousness for and on behalf of every member of your nation and your community and your family. You have a supreme responsibility to amplify that Christ flame, and I know of no better way than in the exercise of the science of the spoken Word.

You have a responsibility to see to it that the knowledge of this karma and also of this teaching is spread abroad throughout the land. You have heard the admonishment to not hide your light under a bushel—that bushel of neglect![8] You cannot sit home on your haunches and there give your decrees and deprive mankind of the knowledge of the law. You must go out into the highways and byways and become teachers of mankind.[9] You must rescue the little children who are born, who come into the schools, and who are programmed away from their immortal destiny. You must take up the cause! You must enter the fray! You must fight the good fight for the Goddess of Liberty.

Remember, I have kept my promise to you this night; I have put you in contact with the teachings. Now I say, will you say no to the Divine Mother? Will you say, "I have forgotten my vow"? Or will you stand up tall, take your responsibility seriously and your word that you gave? Do you not remember that "by thy word thou shalt be justified and by thy word thou shalt be condemned"?[10] So it is written; so it is the law of the judgment.

I remind you that ere a century has passed, all of you will stand before me once again, and you will have in your hands to present to the Lords of Karma the harvest of good work or a crop that has failed. And you will stand alone to give testimony to the Lords of Karma. You will make your report as to the use you have made of this life and this quotient of energy.

And then, if you have not succeeded in earning your ascension, you will be there knocking on the portals of birth. And then you will be faced with that dilemma of a programming of a civilization against the birth of the Christed ones and you will face the karma of your neglect, of your failure to inform the nations of this karma of denying life. So then, the cycles turn quickly. Many are called but few are chosen, and those who choose to be the elect of God are those who win.[11]

I am counting on you, Keepers of the Flame, to be winners in this life! And I back you with the full momentum of my lifestream if you will choose to win for light, for freedom. I thank you, ladies and gentlemen, and I bid you good evening.

Comments by the Messenger Elizabeth Clare Prophet
Following the Goddess of Liberty's Dictation

We express our gratitude to the Goddess of Liberty
for her contact with our hearts and her release of this most
important instruction. It is always a privilege to be in the
presence of the Goddess of Liberty, awakening a devotion
we have to her that spans the ages—her great courage and
strength, her keeping the flame of the Mother that has
welcomed all of us, our ancestors, to this soil. She has held
the immaculate concept for our life, for our nation, for a
destiny throughout the world.

Considering her subject of the bringing-forth of
children, I would like to mention that in *Liberty Proclaims*
she speaks of the edict of the Lords of Karma that was a
staying action on the birth of the fallen ones—very
rebellious lifestreams who were incarnated on Atlantis,
who caused the sinking of Atlantis through their misuses
of the sacred fire, their manipulations of consciousness,
their black magic. These are the souls who were not
allowed to embody until this century, and with them came
the wrath of the drug culture and all types of misuses of
energy.

In *Liberty Proclaims* she sends forth the edict that the
doors are closed to opportunity to these fallen ones to
incarnate until the Christed ones can arrive. So she
proclaims the coming of the light-bearers; and with that
proclamation, made a number of years ago here in this
city, began this programming of zero population growth

and the abortion of those on the way. And so now we are fighting the battle for the very life of the saviours of mankind.

Also included in this book [12] is the vision which the Goddess of Liberty gave to George Washington on the battlefield as he prayed in the cold winter. It was published in 1880 in the *National Tribune,* and the Goddess of Liberty speaks to General Washington as the Son of the Republic. She gives to him the vision of the destiny of America. She shows to him three major wars which will come, and she shows the saving of the nation by the rallying of the people around the banner of unity.

Unity is the angel by the name of Micah; and that wearing of that banner of unity is a familiar sign to Americans because Micah is the angel who led the people of Israel across the wilderness, through the Red Sea, into the Promised Land. Micah—unity—the banner of union! He reminds us in the hour of the struggle, in the hour of the divide-and-conquer tactics of the manipulators, that we are brethren.

In the name of Liberty, I salute you this night then as brothers and sisters of the one flame of freedom. Let us vow before Almighty God that we will never again allow ourselves to be divided by section, by North and South, by hatred, by prejudice, by jealousy or envy, but that we will remain one in the white-fire core of the Christ consciousness.

In conclusion this evening, may we sing the mantra "We are one." Let us affirm the oneness of our hearts united in our dedication to freedom for all mankind; and let us affirm our oneness with the entire Spirit of the Great White Brotherhood, our oneness with the ascended masters, who are so close to us, waiting in the wings of life for us to fulfill our promises. As Robert Frost, the American poet, said, "We have miles to go and promises to keep." To the keeping of our promises, let us keep the flame of life together.

III

Enshrining the Flame of Freedom
in the Capitals of the Nations
by Saint Germain

In the center of the crystal I AM come. And I AM the light of freedom, the light of Aquarius. I have garnered the light of far-off worlds from cosmic beings who have knelt before the throne of Almighty God this day, giving their offering of the flame of the second ray, the ray of wisdom, as a thrust of fire to deliver unto mankind the freedom of their souls' desire.

I AM Saint Germain. I come not alone, but I come with Portia and with these cosmic evolutions who have answered the calls of Keepers of the Flame on Terra who keep the flame of life with Sanat Kumara. These cosmic beings have gone before the Almighty One, Alpha of the sun, to dedicate that portion of their causal bodies so necessary for the salvation of souls and the soul of a planet.

And therefore I come—the bearer of gifts, of dispensations, of fires of freedom not my own, but mine to claim. For I am in the I AM of each one and in the presence of the sun, and I am in the Sun behind the sun of each and every one of you who stands to keep the flame of life this hour. Therefore, let now the cycles roll from the causal bodies of these ones and from freedom's scroll! Let it roll now to implement the fire of freedom!

There are cosmic beings who come wearing the initiatic dress of the peoples of every nation upon Terra. They come for the enshrining of freedom. And this is the quickening fire, the quickening of a flame that has not been quickened in ten thousand years. It is a dispensation of light sent forth to all the nations that souls of light within the nations might respond to the teachings of the I AM THAT I AM vouchsafed unto Moses and to Christ, to Buddha and to Mary, and to sons and daughters of God in this age.

The messengers of God and the holy angels carry in their hearts the sacred fire to ignite the torch of freedom that presents the opportunity of the Four and Twenty Elders,[1] of the flame of the God Star, and of the Lords of Karma for the nations to fulfill their fiery destiny. This places a responsibility upon Keepers of the Flame to carry the torch of freedom to every nation. And I project the vision before you of teaching centers of the white cube of the Church Universal and Triumphant in every nation upon earth, in the capital cities of the world.

And therefore I select the monument, the focal point for the enshrining of freedom; and I place that focus of freedom in the heart of America, in the very heart chakra of the Goddess of Freedom reigning over the Capitol building of the United States. And there the heart chakra of the Divine Mother shall broadcast the fires of freedom from the crystal of the heart, from the twelve fiery focal points of the mandala of her crystal. So shall freedom from the twelve hierarchies of the sun go forth and beam that arc of light to the heart of the Statue of Liberty.

And I place that flame of freedom in the heart of the Statue of Mother Russia so that all peoples in Russia may identify once again with the Mother of the World—the Mother of the World that is not bound by a state or by a government that is not keeping the government of Christ—but that the people might know that the Mother is the deliverer of the nations, that the Mother is the initiator of the nations, that the Mother is the fire of the holy Kumaras, that the crown of the Mother is the crown of life and the starry diadem of life is the bursting-forth of causal bodies of cosmic beings who send forth the ray for the crystallization of the God flame.

I AM freedom. I AM in the heart of freedom. Now let the angels of freedom who have taken their places across the planetary body raise the taper of fire! And at the moment of the invocation of the Elohim given forth by the devotees assembled here in consonance with the angelic hosts, so this conflagration shall be the testimony of the entire Spirit of the Great White Brotherhood—ascended and unascended devotees of fire chanting the name of God as Elohim for the victory of freedom in the freedom's star of Terra that Terra is to be. At the signal, most gracious ladies and gentlemen, will you give with me this chant of the Elohim and feel the fire flow from your heart as you participate in this sacred ritual of igniting the earth for the victory of the age. [Audience chants "Elohim" three times.]

In the Christ of Cuernavaca, in the Christ of the Andes and the Christ of Corcovado, in the Great Pyramid of Egypt, in the heart of the statues of the Buddha in the East, in the Taj Mahal, in the great cathedrals, and in the statues of the great patriots, in the obelisks, in the monuments, so the light of freedom has been implanted as a flame from our hearts—your heart and my heart and the heart of cosmic beings and the heart of Alpha and Omega. So in the chain of hierarchy we are one in the fire of freedom.

And none can stay the hand of the Almighty and none can say to him, "What doest thou?" Who dares to question the will of God or the destiny of the fires of freedom? God is no respecter of persons, [2] and therefore the coming of the Lord is according to the cosmic timetable of the light of Aquarius. Let it blaze! Let it blaze! Let it blaze in the light of freedom's fire!

I speak to every soul on Terra who loves freedom, who enshrines freedom as the fire of be-ness and of creativity in the whole. I speak to every soul: Hear the call of freedom! Feel the flow of freedom! For the Fallen One is bound; the Fallen One has been taken; the Fallen One has stood judgment before the Court of the Sacred Fire. Because of the binding of the Fallen One and the staying action of the carnal mind, you now hear the call to battle, "En garde! Company advance!" Hear the call of the Knight Commander! Hear the call of the general in the field!

Hear the call! For this is the moment to move for the victory of the light in every nation! This is the moment to reverse the tide of darkness! This is the moment to give your invocations to the Great Divine Director! This is the moment to be on your knees in prayer before the living God! This is the moment, this is the time and the space, for the victory!

I AM here and you can see me if you will! I AM here and I give you the fire in your all-seeing eye to perceive that I AM real, that I ensoul the destiny of nations, that I stand behind every freedom-loving soul on Terra. I AM the initiation of cycles in the light of Aquarius. I AM the cosmic consciousness of freedom. I carry the light of the Mother and the book of her law. And I read the law of the Mother daily; for I, too, would commune with God in the scriptures of the Mother of the World.

So hear the call of Alpha! Hear the call of Omega! Hear the light of the Elohim! Elohim! [Chanted by Saint Germain and the audience.] So hear the feminine call unto the Elohim—the call of Portia, my beloved, for cosmic justice and opportunity.

This is the opening of the door, and remember the word "The darkest hour precedes the dawn of victory." Remember the word "Without the crucifixion, there can be no resurrection, no ascension in the fires of God." The crucifixion is the necessary action of the law whereby all things that form a part of that identity that is apart from

God must be placed upon the cross of white fire.

Therefore, the consummation in the fires of love of all self-awareness apart from God—this is the dying on the cross unto life eternal. Let none shrink from this calling. Let none fear or faint walking on the fourteen stations of the cross, for I AM with you. I AM with you in the light of Aquarius—and you will not fail, you will not fail!

O Mother, O children, O children of the sun and Keepers of the Flame, you will not fail; for God is in you! God is in your heart! God is the banner of the soul; God is the engram of light that forms the monogram of your own Electronic Presence. This is invincible light! This is God Mercury and the wings of Sirius! This is the eagle of Libra and the fulfillment of America's destiny in the balance scales of that hierarchy of the sun!

O come into the One! O America, O children of the I AM from every corner of the earth, come into the flame of Liberty! Rise up in the courage and the honor of the Mother! And know you not, blessed children of the Mother, that the activation of the fires of the Mother has produced the pleasure cults and the cults of *hedon* on Terra and the overinvolvement in the misuses of the sacred fire? Let that be cleansed now by the washing of the waters by the Word.[3] Let the flow of Omega now be a torrent of sacred fire to cleanse the consciousness, to erase all that is less than God's desire!

Now I stretch forth my hands to release the energies of the magnet of the Great Central Sun. I magnetize the sacred fire of the Mother flame high unto the altar of the Christ within the heart. Let the energy rise! Let it now be without that disguise of all the misuses and the pornography and the blaspheming of her name. Let that pure stream of energy be stripped of mankind's inharmony! Let it be stripped!

In the name of the living God, I stand before you and I command the flame of the Mother to rise within you—to rise unto the skies to greet the light of the sun of Alpha for the converging of the wholeness of our God. Be free from all carnal desiring! Be free from the beast that ascendeth up out of the bottomless pit of carnal desire! It has no power over the sons and daughters of God who will to be free.

O will to be free, blessed ones! Will you not will to be free? Let your will be full! Let it be generous! Let it be full-blown as the sails of the Niña, the Pinta, and the Santa Maria! For the Holy Spirit requires all of your willing, all of your loving, all of your caring, to carry the ship of the threefold flame into the new world for the founding of the new order of the ages.

And God has blessed your undertaking. He has shined upon it. He has released the light of freedom. So he has sent forth a blessing for the raising-up of the pyramid of life within your heart. Stone by stone, let the pyramid be built—not as an outer symbol or an outer sign—but let the pyramid be within your heart a holy shrine. Let it be dedicated now to the ascension of every man, woman, and child upon this earth.

Let it also be dedicated to the binding of the fallen ones who are the remnants of that Lucifer, the Fallen One. Let them be bound by the action of the sacred fire! You see, when you allow that Mother flame to rise higher and higher, it will claim the victory over the fallen ones. And all of their organizations and their systems and their isms and their nightmares of division—they will go into the flame.

I AM Saint Germain and I proclaim the victory of the light within you! If you would but stand with the same fervor that I am standing, you would see how the enthusiasm and the joy and the light of your hearts would set on fire a world waiting to be set free! And the elementals are longing for that sacred fire which you, and only you, can release from your heart's desire.

O surrender all human desire, all human willing and wishing and the mental aberrations of the human intellect

YOUR DIVINE SELF

Chart of Your Divine Self

There are three figures represented in the chart, which we will refer to as the upper figure, the middle figure, and the lower figure. The upper figure is the I AM Presence, the I AM THAT I AM, God individualized for every son and daughter of the flame. The Divine Monad consists of the I AM Presence surrounded by the spheres (rings of color, of light) which comprise the causal body. This is the body of First Cause that contains within it man's "treasure laid up in heaven"—perfect works, perfect thoughts and feelings, perfect words—energies that have ascended from the plane of action in time and space as the result of man's correct exercise of free will and his correct qualification of the stream of life that issues forth from the heart of the Presence and descends to the level of the Christ Self.

The middle figure in the chart is the mediator between God and man, called the Christ Self, the Real Self, or the Christ consciousness. It has also been referred to as the Higher Mental Body. The Christ Self overshadows the lower self, which consists of the soul evolving through the four planes of Matter in the four lower bodies corresponding to the planes of earth, air, fire, and water; that is, the etheric body, the mental body, the emotional body, the physical body.

The three figures of the chart correspond to the Trinity of Father (the upper figure), Son (the middle figure), and Holy Spirit (the lower figure), which the evolving soul is intended to become and for whom the body is the temple. The lower figure is the nonpermanent aspect of being which is made permanent through the ritual of the ascension. The ascension is the process whereby the lower figure, having balanced his karma and fulfilled his divine plan, merges first with the Christ consciousness and then with the living Presence of the I AM THAT I AM. Once the ascension has taken place, the soul, the corruptible aspect of being, becomes the incorruptible one, a permanent atom in the body of God. The Chart of Your Divine Self is therefore a diagram of yourself—past, present, and future.

The lower figure represents mankind evolving in the planes of Matter. This is how you should visualize yourself standing in the violet flame, which you invoke in the name of the I AM Presence and in the name of the Christ in order to purify your four lower bodies in preparation for the ritual of the alchemical marriage—your soul's reunion with the Spirit, the I AM Presence. The lower figure is surrounded by a tube of light, which is projected from the heart of the I AM Presence in answer to your call. It is a field of fiery protection sustained in Spirit and in Matter for the sealing of the identity of the overcomer. The threefold flame within the heart is the spark of life projected from the I AM Presence through the Christ Self and anchored in the etheric planes in the heart chakra for the purpose of the soul's evolution in Matter. Also called the Christ flame, the threefold flame is the spark of man's divinity, his potential for Godhood.

The crystal cord is the stream of light that descends from the heart of the I AM Presence through the Christ Self, thence to the four lower bodies to sustain the soul's vehicles of expression in time and space. It is over this cord that the energy of the Presence flows, entering the being of man at the top of the head and providing the energy for the pulsation of the threefold flame and the physical heartbeat. When a round of the soul's incarnation in Matter-form is complete, the I AM Presence withdraws the crystal cord, the threefold flame returns to the level of the Christ, and the energies of the four lower bodies return to their respective planes.

The dove of the Holy Spirit descending from the heart of the Father is shown just above the head of the Christ. When the individual man, as the lower figure, puts on and becomes the Christ consciousness as Jesus did, the descent of the Holy Spirit takes place and the words of the Father, the I AM Presence, are spoken, "This is my beloved Son in whom I AM well pleased" (Matt. 3:17).

A more detailed explanation of the Chart of Your Divine Self is given in the Keepers of the Flame Lessons and in *Climb the Highest Mountain* by Mark and Elizabeth Prophet, published by The Summit Lighthouse.

and that stubborn human will! Let it go into the flame!
How long will you, children of the One, make the
ascended masters do battle with your own carnal mind and
your own stubbornness? It is yours to overcome! We have
overcome our own.

Now enter the fray and slay that beast! Slay that
beast, I say, of the Fallen One within! And be free! Be free
to be world conquerors! Will you not be enticed by my
offer this day? Will you not be magnetized by Saint
Germain's ray? Will you not see that the ascended masters
are real, that we stand in life this hour, that because we
stand in your nation's capital, America still stands?

Do you think that the puny mortals who have taken
their positions in this government have the capability to
hold together America as the greatest nation upon earth? I
can tell you they are sorely lacking! They are a poor excuse
for God-government. And the few who have the honor of
true patriots, patrons, and patriarchs of the law are not
enough to hold the balance of the light.

We commend those who strive for freedom. And we
say: Because we back you this day, America will not go
down with the setting sun, but she will rise with the dawn.
She will rise in the light of Aries to manifest the Christ
consciousness. She will rise, then, to that capstone in the
pyramid of life; and each and every one who claims that
capstone as his own will also rise in the victory of the
ascension.

I AM Saint Germain. I have enshrined freedom in the
capitals of the nations this day. Now I enshrine freedom in
the soul, freedom in the heart, of every Keeper of the
Flame. Receive that fire, O devotees of the One! Receive
it now and be infired! Take your places in the mandala of government! You are needed in the service of the
light. Therefore, serve the Mother in the government of
your nation. Serve the Mother in the mandala of the
City Foursquare. Take your place! Release the light!
Release the music of the spheres! And let balance be the

harmony which impels the victory.

I salute you—heart, head, and hand! I salute you in the flame that is our victory! Victory in America! Victory in the glory of Old Glory! Victory in the fifty stars that are for the test of the ten in the five secret rays! Yes, let America be on her knees this day in prayer for the nations of the world! So let it come to pass that by the victory of the Christ consciousness within you, the flame of freedom shall burn on! Terra shall become freedom's star, and her evolutions shall rise invincible in the ascension, invincible in the skies.

I AM Saint Germain in the heart of freedom in every nation. I stand! I AM! I remain!

IV

Obedience Is Better than Sacrifice
by the Ascended Master Godfre

Good evening, ladies and gentlemen. I salute you in the flame of God-obedience. I welcome you to the altar where the flame of obedience burns brightly, consuming your sacrifice of all that is less than the Christ consciousness.

For the action of the light, for the release of the law of being, obedience is better than sacrifice.[1] Those who substitute sacrifice for obedience will find themselves outside the center of our oneness when we come to claim our own. Obedience is a flame imparted from the heart of God to the heart of man. It is the flame whereby the soul finds its cosmic dimension, wherein the soul can reach for that consciousness of congruency with the blueprint of life.

To quote an expression of your own, mankind are "out of whack." They are not aligned or attuned with the inner fires of life. Their four lower bodies are askew; and the wedges of darkness projected by the fallen ones in their discord, in their manipulations, separate the flow of light from the within to the without. Therefore, men and women who live on the periphery of existence do not experience the great reservoir of light that flows within, that burns on—burns on as the crystal river of living flame.

And thus a surface consciousness does not satisfy the craving of the soul for the immortal reunion. The craving of the soul for the entering-in to the oneness of life is translated through the labyrinth of the carnal mind to the outer senses, to the outer desires; and therefore we see that the downfall of nations is the endless pursuit of pleasure and a pleasure cult by a people who are yearning for the flow of the life of the Mother—Mother Liberty and her torch held high, the Mother of Cycles, Mary the Mother of the Christed one.

Come then, children of the sun! I would give you contact with the inner flame. I would let you sense, by a fragrance of that flame, your own communion with the inner geometry of being. I would reestablish the flow of the movement of consciousness—not to the gratification of outer desire, but to the fulfillment of the inner light.

It is the desiring of the soul for wholeness that has prompted the Christed ones of the ages to move to the center of life no matter what the cost or what the pain or what the sacrifice. Yes, obedience is better than sacrifice; but the sacrifice of the lesser self is a part of the call of obedience. For how can you be obedient to the will of God when the bag and baggage of the world is in the way? You must be free to run, to move in the wind, to answer the call of hierarchy for the saving of a nation.

Those who understand the building of a nation, the building of a golden age, count not the cost. For they have seen the vision of the future. They have seen generations unborn coming into the awareness of the God consciousness and of liberty. They have also seen the vision of darkness; they have seen the vision of the compromise; they have seen what will take place in America and on Terra if they do not make right choices in this hour.

I would give you of my flame, of the inner ear, the hearing ear that hears the voice of God. I would give you the consciousness of the sound ray and of the light ray that is contact with our hierarchy of light. Let your inner ear be quickened then by mighty Cosmos' secret rays, that you might hear the voice of the Son of God, your own Christ Self, that you might hear and live—that you might hear and live to respond to the command "Be ye therefore perfect, even as your Father which is in heaven is perfect."[2]

I am a God-free being because I have willed to be free in God. You can be free if you will it so. But I point out that your freedom cannot be won either at the expense of society or in neglect of civilization. Freedom is the parallel lines of individual self-mastery and planetary self-mastery. There is no such thing as individual self-mastery that is won without concern for humanity. The implementation of the salvation of a planet comes about because individuals care enough for one another, because individuals are willing to lay down their life that others might take it and live.

The selflessness that we speak of in sacrifice is not the canceling-out of self. It is truly that enlightened self-interest whereby you champion the light of the Christ where you are and through that light you reclaim that Christ for every living soul. You cannot win alone, but you must be all-one in God in order to manifest the victory for others.

Therefore, keep the flame of the citadel of your consciousness; and be ashamed to go to sleep at night if you have not meditated upon the balance of your inner flame and the alignment of your four lower bodies to that flame. And as you pass into sleep, realize that you are a reflecting pool reflecting the light of the inner sun of God. Through the night and through the day, you are the authority of the law living beneath that rod. You are the equation of being; you are the multiplication factor for the generation of the Christ consciousness in society that will bring about the regeneration of the God consciousness in all mankind.

Toe the mark, disciples of the Christ! Toe the mark, I say! Contact the God Star! Reach for that God Star Sirius

and let the Four and Twenty Elders who sit in judgment at
the Court of the Sacred Fire release their energies through
you that you might be an electrode for the expansion of
the flame in this hour, in this hour that can be the victory
of life on earth.[3]

How well I remember when the blessed ascended
master Saint Germain took me to the Royal Teton Retreat
prior to my ascension during that period in my last incarnation of preparation for the messengership representing
the Great White Brotherhood. How well I remember
seeing the portent of the future, of what the future might
be in America—the projection of the ascended masters'
consciousness for the golden-age society.

The vision of that victory, the vision of prophecy of a
golden age to be born in this land, was based on the
premise of certain numbers among this mighty people who
would respond to the teachings of their own I AM Presence
and to the law of the violet flame, to the law of the One.
That promise was based upon the projection of an
equation, a mathematical equation, of souls in incarnation
and souls who would take incarnation—souls who would
vow to keep the flame of life through the giving of decrees
for America and the world.

Now we have seen in the passing of the decades that
many who vowed to keep that flame, to lay the foundation
for the golden age, have departed from the teaching of the
law of the One, have departed from the giving of decrees,
and have entered into all manner of psychic manifestation,
psychic involvement, the flattery of the ego, and the
contact of those discarnates who impersonate the ascended
masters. Those who were intended to take embodiment in
these decades to fulfill this law of the One and to lay the
foundation—many of these have come. But many have
been denied entrance through the portals of birth—not by
the Lords of Karma, but by mankind's free will.

Therefore, the Council of the Royal Teton, in
reviewing this week the fiery destiny of America and its

fulfillment, sends through me a report to the Keepers of the Flame that you would understand that there is in this moment a gap in the plan of hierarchy. That gap has been created by the division projected by the fallen ones and the black magicians and the misuse of the Mother flame in witchcraft. That gap is the separation of the I AM students—those who have the law—from those who are seizing the light of the law through this messenger, through the Mother flame. And therefore the body of God who has the God consciousness of the I AM THAT I AM is divided on Terra, and you know a house divided against itself cannot stand. [4]

I call forth the flame of the God Star Sirius for enlightenment to those who serve in the name of Godfre, in the name of Lotus, and in the name of the I AM Presence! I call forth that light, that sacred fire, to cut across now those forcefields of hypnotic control by the fallen ones who would keep the flow of this energy from those who have the inheritance of the law and the teaching.

I place before you the understanding that this gap has also been caused by the fact that many who began in the Path through this activity and through the I AM activity have not stayed steadfast on the Path; for they have entered into the condemnation of the messengers or they have entered into the pride of the ego, its ambition, or into the action of discouragement through cynicism, through the weight of world consciousness. Again, a contributing factor to the gap is that those souls intending to incarnate are waiting in the wings for the joyous reception of the chelas of the ascended masters who will welcome them into homes of light.

Now I place before the student body the need to give fervent invocations for and on behalf of those souls of light who have taken their inner vows, who will be willing to serve the flame—one in mind and heart and soul, one in the flame of the entire Spirit of the Great White

Brotherhood. Let them be cut free then by your calls and by our answers! Let them be cut free by the Elohim Astrea from all that which causes a lack of discernment, a lack of discrimination of the true and the false vibrations of the ascended hierarchy.

And now let the organ at Shigatse roll from the Master Kuthumi! Let the rolling of the chords of the great organ of life be for the playing of the symphonies unto the children—souls of God who shall come forth because there is even now rippling across Terra a response of love and obedience to love above and beyond the compromises of those who would manipulate world population trends to their own designs. And so let the chords of the grand organ of the Master of Life now be heard by parents and children. Let these chords be heard and let them be for the sealing of life.

I place my flame of God-obedience for the protection of the incoming souls. And they shall come! For I shall stand! For I AM the guard; I AM the purity of the cosmic honor flame. I take my stand with Saint Germain as the minuteman of the hour. I take my stand to guard the consciousness of the purity of lifewaves.

Will you take your stand with me? Will you stand with purity, with God consciousness, with the Goddess of Light, the Queen of Light, the Goddess of Purity? Will you place now the authority of your rod firmly in the ground as a Moses, as a Joshua, as a leader of the children of light? Will you carry the shepherd's crook of Peter and of the Vicar of Christ? Will you carry the authority that will clear the way for the lambs of God?

I am projecting to you the great glory of the coming of the Christed ones in this year 1976. I am projecting for you now, through the instruments of the Royal Teton and the great mirror there, that vision of America—glorious, victorious, in a golden age of enlightenment and peace. I place this vision in the etheric plane, in the mental plane; and I turn over to the Mother the key for the passing of this vision into the plane of water and earth, into the cycles of Omega. May she then take from her heart this key of life, this key to the mystery of life, and impart it to the devotees that they might complete those spirals begun in our octaves of light, released from the heart of the Great Divine Director and from the heart of Saint Germain, fulfilling the edict of an age, fulfilling the light of the Holy Spirit.

O America, let the very soil of this nation now glow in the fiery crystal of the violet flame! Let the rocks and the earth and the vegetation and the life of a people be saturated from the violet fire that ascends from the sun of even pressure in the heart of the earth, saturating the four quadrants with the light of the holy of holies. I AM a God-free being. I pass to you the torch of your God-freedom. I anchor within your heart the rose of your own unfolding cosmic consciousness. By obedience to the inner law of the design of life, you, too, can become God-free!

And I have the joy of the dispensation, the opportunity, to one day welcome you to the ranks of the immortals. And in the hour of your ascension, I shall stand upon the mountain and I shall hand to you the crystal cup of the elixir of life. And you shall drink of that cup—and you will feel the charge of your own God Presence, the charge of the ascension flame of Serapis Bey and the mighty seraphim of life! And you will feel the tingling of the light as atoms and cells within you receive the currents of the ascension flame rising from beneath your feet, the threefold flame of life intensifying the action until your four lower bodies are enveloped in the light of ascension's fires. And you shall rise from the summit of life, from the mountains of North America and from the Temple at Luxor—rise into the arms of your own God Presence.

Keepers of the Flame, you are destined to immortality! You are destined to the ascension! And I will come to you in the hour already known by your God Presence to give you that passing of the arc of life, to send you on your way to cosmic consciousness and individuality in God sealed forevermore. Yes, I will come for you.

I proclaim to you your birthday in the light, your natal day of freedom. And I say to you, see to it that your soul does not take flight unless you have planted firmly in this soil that focus of your flame, that focus of victory and of freedom's name! Dare not leave this earth without leaving behind you those footprints in the sands of life. Dare not leave Terra until you have made a contribution of cosmic worth, until you have opened the door for children and souls of light to take up your torch.

And until there is one, one chela in the law, who can take your momentum and your mantle, you must remain with Terra. You must stay until there is a runner who will run with the same speed of victory with which you run. And therefore, learn to be the instrument of the cosmic teachers. Learn to pass that torch of consciousness, of your fervor as patriots in this land and every land—patriots focusing the love for the inner mandala of the nations, patriots focusing love for Saint Germain, the patriot of every age. O children of the sun, do you not understand that you must leave upon Terra a way out for souls yearning to be free? You dare not, you must not, seek that ascension except on the parallel line of imparting to all the same God-mastery that is in your heart.

O precious ones, hear my plea! The children of the world are waiting for the teaching of the law. Now go forth! Go forth in the flame of the fatherhood, the motherhood of God. Go forth to contact the soldiers waiting in the field, waiting for the coming of the general, waiting for the command of God. They seek the leadership that you have! They seek the Word. They seek the sure and certain trumpet of the Lord. They hear the march of victory, they hear the triumphal march; and they look for those who will lead them to the Source, lead them to the One, lead them to the ascended masters.

This land is the land of violet fire. This land is the land of freedom's desire. This land is the land filled with people who love the light. This is a land filled with people who are lost in the night. I say, go out and find them! Go out and claim them! For this is the land of the Virgin's light. This is the land of the Woman clothed with the Sun.[5] This is the land of the light that will make all nations one—one in the light of Maitreya, one in the light of the law of God within the hearts of those who are the real, who are the accomplished, who are the dedicated ones of old.

I call you forth, children of the sun, from the golden-age civilizations of old! I quicken your memory of that golden age in the Sahara. I quicken your memory of South America and of the buried cities of the Amazon. Now then, come with me in my mantle of light as I take you this night as your souls go into the realm of sleep. So as your souls go forth from your body temples to keep the flame of life, come with me as I show you the records of those ancient times. Come with me as I show you what we have done together for the light.

For what we have done we can do again—we shall do again! We *shall* be the fulfillment of victory in this age! We cannot fail, for Saint Germain is our love and our calling. We must not fail him. We dare not fail him! No, we shall never turn back until we have fulfilled the love of the Master of Freedom. To him I pledge my heart, my head, my hand. And to all of you who keep that flame, I pledge my support of the flame of God-obedience. Claim it in the hour of the testing! Claim it in the hour of the temptation! Claim it in the hour of the victory, and I shall be there kneeling beside you, interceding with God on behalf of the obedience of your soul.

In the flame of love, I proclaim to you now that goal. Obedience is better than sacrifice. Now take that flame! Run with it! And see what you can become for America, for the world, for souls waiting for the bursting in the sky of the nova of your light consciousness, waiting for your attainment that they might attain in your footsteps—souls waiting for your mantle, for your example, for your response to your God-ability.

Go forth now, sons and daughters of Liberty! Be the flame of light to all and let life quench the darkness of all death. I AM life! I AM alive forevermore. I AM in the consciousness of America for the celebration of victory, victory, victory!

V

The Precipitation of the Diamond of the Will of God
by El Morya

Hail, sons and daughters of flame! I come from Darjeeling to salute you in the flame of life. I come with a will and with a way. I come in destiny's fire and I come in victory's light. I come in the momentum of freedom from the heart of Saint Germain. I come from the Darjeeling Council table, where we are gathered in contemplation of the diamond heart of the Mother of the World. I come from deliberations concerning the problems of earth and the dilemma of the nations, where we have discussed the matter of light and darkness and the concealment of the dark ones from before the face of the children of the sun.

We come then, as usual, on our rescue mission, calling souls to separate out from the darkness of their own subconscious, to come out and separate from that labyrinth of the carnal mind. We come with the star before us. We come with the diamond of God's will. We come to fulfill the precipitation of that diamond, and we look for the place to anchor that fire and that flame of devotees of the will of God.

We scan the centuries and we scan the light of chelas. We scan those who would be chelas but say they cannot. We look for will. We look for the momentum of the will to be. We look for those who have the courage to fling themselves into the majesty of overcoming, into the way of life victorious. We look for those who understand the light of service as the perpetual motion of the light-bearers. We look for those whose heads are not cast down, but who look into the skies to see the stars and to see in the stars the hope of life and life everlasting.

You have heard of the cracking of the whip of the Darjeeling Trailblazer. Well, I am blazing a trail today, and I am going from city to city to see who I will find who is ready to receive the precipitation of the diamond of the will of God, who is ready to make room in the inn of being for the light of that will, who is ready to make the sacrifice to make a home of light for Saint Germain and the chelas of Saint Germain.

Who are the chelas of Saint Germain? Well, after the spanking that I gave to the children of the light through the Mother in my last dictation,[1] I come with the joyous announcement that some of the chelas who have been spanked have now been received by Saint Germain as chelas. Now don't you think it was worthwhile to be spanked in order to be received by the Lord of the Seventh Ray? Now we see what Saint Germain has in store for those who will to be in the light of the fire of God's will.

And so once again, in such a short time, we have some vacant seats in Darjeeling, for souls have gone forth to be trained of Saint Germain. And Saint Germain is not content to train the souls in the etheric retreats of the Great White Brotherhood. No, he is determined to have the focuses such as the focus of the Master of Paris—a home of light in the physical octave, a home of light in the cities, a home of light where souls can be received.

So then, where are the stalwart ones, where are the builders, where are the pioneers who will have the courage to enter the canyons of New York City and Chicago and all of the great cities of America and the world? Onward, marching, marching come the angels of light! They come then to announce to souls of Morya: "Now take flight in the eagle wings of Sirius! Follow the light of the new day! Follow the light of the seventh ray!"

Now understand why I say that there is a need for greater and greater intensification of the light of the violet flame. For the light of the violet flame is clearing a way, carving a tunnel, into the depths of the astral. Why are we carving a tunnel? Because there be some souls in the darkness this night who have heard the decrees of the students, who have called out to God: "Save me, O my God! For I would come forth from the depths of darkness and I would join the decreers on Terra!"

So your calls are echoing through the planes of Mater! And so we say, keep on keeping on! Keep on invoking the violet flame! For there are souls in the corridors of memory whom you have known long, long ago; and some of these souls are tied to you by love and others by karma and others by the imbalance of injustice.

They are tugging on your garments; and you will find, as you attempt to ascend to the heights of the mountains, that the souls tugging in the large cities of the world will pull you back even as they pulled back Gautama from nirvana. Back he came, the Enlightened One. He could not stay in meditation in the holy of holies; but he returned from out the Great Silence to answer the call of souls—souls yearning to be free, souls having an awareness of a destiny and seeing the enlightened ones climbing to the summit of life.

Remember then the words of Jesus to Peter, who said unto him: "Quo vadis? Where are you going, Lord?" And unto him, the chela of the Christ, the Lord declared, "I go to Rome to be crucified again, to be placed on the cross of white fire." And Peter knew that his Lord could be crucified only through him, only through his sacrifice of that human will, that stubbornness, that rebellion against the diamond of the will of God.

And back he went—back to the home of light, back

to that center—to be crucified for his Lord. And that sacrifice of the one chosen to be the Vicar of Christ is the rock upon which the Church is built.[2] Each time a soul sacrifices the lesser self to the greater cause of world good will, upon that rock we build. We build unto the stars; we connect souls in the depths of darkness to the star of the I AM Presence.

Let the light of souls then be known. And let it be known that the chelas of Saint Germain have the assignment, as their initiation in the seventh ray, to meet the public, to meet the world, to meet the people—the displaced persons, the pure sons and daughters of God— to meet them in the cities and in the country, in the highways and the byways, to talk to the children of the light and to talk to the children of the One. And so you will find that Saint Germain will demand proof that you have been a chela of Morya—not a carrying card and not a badge, but proof, invincible proof, that the will of God is the diamond fiery core of the precipitation of the holy amethyst, of the violet flame that is freedom shooting forth from centers of light.

Now let us see how you will rescue mankind from their plight! Let us see whether chelas of Morya will be worthy of the name as they go forth all life to claim. Let us see now; let us see what we shall see. And those of you who were left outside of the Retreat of Good Will may be invited now to come inside to see if you will instill God's will as the diamond heart of Mary.

Now look again and see the teacher in the Darjeeling Council chambers! See who is teaching the class in good will. It is Mary the Mother—the hope, the joy, the crown of the will of God, the devotion to the blueprint of life. And so the Mother comes to discipline those chelas who would not succumb to the light of Morya. Now let us see if the diamond heart of Mary can woo you to surrender that human will.

Come then—new chelas, old chelas! Come to touch

the hem of the garment of the Mother of the World. It is a blue garment of her love; it is the mantle of the Christmas Mother. And her children in this year of the Holy Spirit are the devotees of the flame.

And you know, they come from mosques and temples. Be not surprised who you will meet in the Temple of Good Will; for there are many, many who are in the mosques of the East and in the cathedrals of the West and in their temples chanting the name of the Lord God of Israel, chanting the name of Allah. Those who come from near and far—they have this one thing in common: a fierce devotion to the will of God. Yet not all know how to surrender that lesser devotion to the moon of the human will. And therefore, when the sun is in the zenith of the sky, their devotion to the will is high. But in the night hours when the moon sheds the silvery light, they are polarized to that substance of karma, that energy misqualified.

And for that purpose, the Mother of the World comes—the one who has placed the moon beneath her feet.[3] She comes to show the devotees how to conquer self, how to conquer will, how to make that coal of untransmuted substance the diamond—the flawless diamond of the will of God. Now let us see how, one by one, you will take that substance and form the crystals that you will offer unto me and to Maitreya, who will lead you in the path of initiation.

Truly the year 1976 is the year of initiation. I suggest that you form your queue, that you place yourselves one by one in earnest in a line of cosmic consciousness to apply to the Holy Mother and her holy will to receive the anointing that is for the initiation of the light within your chakras. And the Great Divine Director is ready to release spirals of initiation.

And this is the conclusion of the Darjeeling Council as we watch a world moving, as it were, downward, downward in the spirals of no-return. As we watch these momentums, we counteract with an upward spiral and a challenge that we fling into the teeth of the chelas! We must counteract that quicksand movement of the pull of the fallen ones who think that they have the world by the tail. I tell you, they think that they are cloaked somehow in the invisible mantle reserved for the masters. Our eye is on the Illuminati. We watch those who usurp the light of the Christ; and we say, "He who laughs last, laughs best."

And with a twinkle in my eye, I call the chelas: Now rise, I say! I demand it of you! I will not let you remain on that ladder of comfortability where you have placed yourself with your arms folded, saying: "I have reached a place of security. I will rest awhile." Oh, no, you won't— not as long as I am on Terra! Not as long as I am Morya! And not as long as you call to me in love as you have this night and as you do with the fervor of the chelas of freedom and of will. No, I say! I will goad you, I will spur you! I will treat you as my favorite Arabian horse! Yes, I will! I will come to you and I will give you that goad to life and to victory.

I tell you, for every fallen one who has assumed a role in darkness and in the shadows of the vast complex of the governments of the nations, I must have a chela who will rise correspondingly high into the skies, into the star of the I AM Presence. Where are you, O chelas—you who should be here? I speak to you also! I rebuke you for your fear, your cowardice, your waywardness, your willy-nilly, will-o'-the-wisp consciousness! I rebuke you for flirting with death and darkness and self-destruction! I will have you, too, for my chela. I will draw you into the flame.

Watch and see, for the game is not yet over. And we will see who will dare play chess with Morya, who will not confess the secrets of the heart, who will not come forth and reveal the truth of life—all of truth, the shame and the glory as well. Let them come forth! Let them be revealed! Let them go into the flame! Yes, I will have my chelas for initiation. I will move you so long as there is life to be moved.

And I speak to chelas stalwart who are on beds of pain and beds of death. I speak to each and every one, for I am the comfort of the will of God. I will not leave you. How can I leave thee? I love thee! I love thee! I cannot leave thee, O my chelas! You are my heart and my soul. You are my love and my goal. I will take you in my arms. I will carry you across the rapids of life. I will bring you to the throne of God if you have but half a will and if you are willing to give the word of truth and the fiats of the light.

Do you not know, O precious ones, how precious you are to the masters in Darjeeling? How we love to gaze upon that countenance uplifted in the love of earth, in the love of humanity! For all your striving and your serving, I am grateful in the will—in the diamond will of Morya. Now note that the hardness of that diamond is not a hardness of heart, but it is love congealed to cut through the most dense astral substance for the rescuing of life. We come to rescue life. We know the toiling of the carnal mind and the resistance of that mind to the fulfillment of his will. Therefore, we take a certain amount of childishness; but we must put an end to childishness. We must silence that childishness and make it childlike innocence in the heart of a Mother.

Children, wake up! *Wake up,* I say! While the rats eat away at the granary of America, you cannot stay where you are. The caravan of Morya must move on! It must go up the mountain. Hear the cracking of the whip, for I come blazing a trail of light! I will say it again: I must have a chela, a devotee, to counteract the points of darkness for every fallen one who would claim the light and the heritage of America and of the nations of the world. I must have a devotee willing to counteract twenty-four hours a day the darkness of that wicked one.

Now take your assignments; take them. My angels write them for you. Your orders are given. Read them well. I place before your soul and your Christ Self the name of one whose darkness you must counteract. That name will remain with you until you have, by your causal body and by your momentum of light, counteracted that one. And then we will wink the eye at one another and we will say "Checkmate!" We will say "Checkmate!" We will say "Checkmate!" And the victory will be unto the diamond of the will of God *that is you!*

In the love of Saint Germain, in the love of the chelas of the flame, I remain Morya.

VI

America in 1976
by Saint Germain

Hail, sons and daughters of freedom! I AM come in the flame with a fervor for the cause of righteousness. I AM come in the flame of freedom and I look up to the new birth of America.

I look up to the rebirth in the Mother light. I look to the crystal stars of purity. I look to the backdrop of the will of God. I see the body and the blood of Christ as these have been assimilated by sons and daughters of God on this soil; and I see Old Glory as my vision of the future of America—as the new race of light-bearers of which you are the avant-garde. I am welcome here and I thank you for your welcome. I thank you for your hearts afire with freedom, determined to pass that torch of freedom and to continue the light, light, light!

I am in the joy, I am in the ecstasy of communion in the Holy Spirit and in the fire of the all-seeing eye, the very capstone of the pyramid of this experiment in hierarchy. I see the God-design for America, and I see that men and women such as yourselves have held the vision and that this vision, as the hope in the eye of the Mother, will be born if you are faithful to the flame.

The faithfulness of Keepers of the Flame is a joy to

the ascended hosts. And that faithfulness was never more necessary than it is in the coming year. Crosscurrents of the old and the new will mark 1976 as the final hours of the birthday cycle are spent. These hours provide opportunity for an extraordinary transmutation of past momentums that must be cleared.

So let there be the clearing of the decks of the ship of America! Let her decks be cleared and let the Divine Mother and her children walk those decks as they walk the path of initiation! Let them feel the presence of Maitreya and the Cosmic Christ over this land! How appropriately he has sent forth his call to those who would be initiated in light. We initiate a cycle of light and we must perforce intensify that light within you; for this light must swallow up the darkness that the child, America, might be born again.

I ask you then to see the weaving of forces and force-fields. I ask you to anticipate the crosscurrents. I ask you then to take the Holy Child in your arms and carry the child across the turbulent waters. I ask you to be Christ-bearers for America. I ask you, precious ones, to remember that this is the culmination of all that we have given forth in this century—the teachings of the I AM, the understanding of the Mother ray, the glorious mission of the messengers who have come forth to represent our cause.

All of this has been in preparation for this moment when we knew the cycles would turn and when that darkness—that darkness overcoming the land that was a part of the final decade before the birthday—would be broken by the light of the appearing of the Christed one bursting through those clouds of darkness and revealing, according to the timetable of the cosmic clock, that true teaching of the Manchild.

It is the child who will lead America into the future. It is the children who are among you; it is the child of your heart; it is the innocence. America is the land where youth excel, where youth can move forward and lead a nation. O precious ones, gather the youth into your homes! Gather them into your arms and deposit within their hearts your love for Christ and Buddha.

Oh, people of all ages and all whom I address here, you are the youth of America, for you are the new vine! You are the green shoots. You have come forth with the light of the Spirit. You are the hope of the spring. You are the full blossoming of summer and you are the firstfruits of autumn. You are the white-fire core of winter. You are the hope of Liberty as she stands in New York Harbor. You are the hope of the Lady with the Lamp as she looks to see who will come to this land each day. As she sends forth the ray of welcome, her gaze is also upon the Keepers of the Flame who hold that torch high with her.

O Liberty, how we love thee! O Mother of the Flame, O Mother of Lights! O Mother of the Oneness of Starry Heights! O Mother of the Crown of Life! O Mother, O Mother, thou who art the figure of the Lamb's wife![1] O Mother of the Flame, O Mother of the Age! O Liberty, let thy light now grace these chosen ones as they choose to receive all who come to these shores with the fiery destiny locked within their hearts and with God-determination!

I come then to give to you a blueprint etched in a crystal cube—a blueprint for patterned destiny for America in 1976. I place it now within your hearts, for where else can the ascended masters place their treasures but in the hearts of their chelas?

I say to you that by your fervent calls, changes must take place swiftly. There must be withdrawn from the government those individuals who are not serving the light of the Christ. There must be daily invocations made for the elections, for the Christed ones to take office, for the ascended masters' candidates to be relieved of all burden of opposition through the media, through the carnal mind.

Keepers of the Flame, you have a vast responsibility in this year. And only by concerted effort, by self-discipline, will the light flow through you that will be the holding light, the staying power, the holding of America when, in this hour of the passing of the torch, all of the fallen ones will look to dash that cup of the new wine of the Spirit before it reaches America on her birthday, July 4, 1976.

I call every Keeper of the Flame! I call you to the nation's capital! I call you to come and to enshrine the flame of freedom. I call you to come to intensify the action of the violet flame that we might have the energy to use against those individuals of darkness and those movements, the fallen ones who plot all types of disturbances and even the overthrow of the government or the presidency and even the Supreme Court.

There are always the fallen ones who come to prevent the celebration of the victory. I am certain that by the authority of the God within you, they will have no power. And I am just as certain that that authority must be placed as you place yourselves in physical manifestation in the capital city, that it must be manifest there and that you must give your all to this victory.

It is a year of change, a year of movement, a year when you must call forth the stabilization of the armed forces and the defense of America, when you must call to the legions of Archangel Michael and the Four Beings of the Elements to reinforce the defenses of America. Jealousy is a deadly opposition; and it is jealousy in the world powers that causes them to come as vultures to tear from America her abundance, her very flesh, her very life flow. Yes, and those who are in America today are not alert to this desecration of the Mother flame.

Let us look then at the new year as twelve months of victory for the flame of freedom—freedom in God-power, freedom in God-love, freedom in God-mastery, freedom in God-control, freedom in God-obedience and freedom in God-wisdom, freedom in God-harmony, freedom in God-gratitude, freedom in God-justice, freedom in God-reality, freedom in God-vision, and freedom in God-victory.

Let us see these months as the coming of the consciousness of God as Father and as Christed one, as Mother and as Holy Spirit. Let us see it as the year when the Lord Christ inaugurates the flame of the Holy City and lays the foundation of the precipitation of that City Foursquare in the City of the Angels.[2] Let us see it as a year when souls of light worked diligently to demagnetize the universities and colleges, high schools and elementary schools, of the nefarious doctrines of the fallen ones with their nihilism, their cynicism, their atheism, and their materialism devoid of the Spirit.

Let us see this as the year of the crystallization of the God flame in America. And for that flame to crystallize, we must clear the way. We must be the street sweepers. We must be the ones who cleanse and purify. So let 1976 be the year when the seven vials of the violet flame are poured out from Zadkiel's retreat! You have but to intensify your calls to the violet flame to receive this dispensation. It is waiting; it is yours for the asking. It is yours to drink of the wine of the Holy Spirit.

I say, precious ones, the need for the violet flame is great. You must give as much violet flame as you give all other decrees. You must supplement your decrees with the violet flame and with quick calls as you move here and there. Your mantra to the violet flame "America is a land of violet fire—America is the purity God desires!" must be your mantra for the birthday year. And you must see it appear here and there and everywhere, naming the cities, naming the places, and naming yourself.

See yourself as a being of violet fire! See yourself as the purity God desires! See yourself walking the streets, walking the great cities of America, dispensing the violet flame as Christ would do. See yourself in garments of purple and violet and pink! See yourself saturated as a pillar of violet fire!

We must have this cleansing! We must have it; for this is the open door, the opportunity for the clearing of those records which must not be a part of the new foundation of the new age. And never was there a time in all of her history that America could have so much redemption, so much regeneration, so much transmutation of all that is past.

Be free, O mother! Be free, O daughter! Be free, children! Be free, O father! Be free, brothers and sisters! This is the hour of your freedom! Claim it within your soul! As Los Angeles is the soul chakra of California, so Los Angeles is the soul chakra of America. And here the souls of a people will hear the call of the mother who is free, the father who is free, the children who are free.

Understand that freedom must move. Freedom must be known throughout the land and the joy of freedom must dispel every weight and burden. We look to you and to all Keepers of the Flame who will receive this dictation as a letter from me so that they may begin the very first weeks of the new year to translate my directives into action, that we do not lose the cycle of Capricorn to initiate cycles of God-direction in freedom.

O God-direction, O master! O Great Divine Director, now lower into our midst this vast mandala of America and of the golden age! Let it be lowered as a great filigreed canopy of golden light, the golden carving of the angels who come to tell and to foretell of this vision of a golden age that is yet to be.

Beloved ones, we see all. You would be dismayed to see what we see; and therefore, though we see all, we do not tell all. For we see above all the victorious power of the light! We see the victorious power of the violet flame and the light of Astrea as Astrea consecrates her circle and sword of blue flame to the victory of America in this year.

We see the crown of the World Mother. We see the dancing of the flame and the dewdrops and the flowers and the children coming. And so ours is not to paint a picture of the darkness that has covered the land and the influences of darkness and of the fallen ones. Ours is to paint the picture of the rainbow of eternal promise that you might look into the vision of our causal bodies and see that "with God all things are possible."[3]

I recall now Valley Forge. I recall the war for the independence of the colonies. I recall that revolution reversing the course of the karma of Europe which the dark ones would have placed upon America by entanglement, by association, by taxation. And I see the great vision and the diamond light of the mind of George Washington, who by the thrust of the mind of God became the white-fire core reversing that energy back to that shore from whence it came.

I see him kneeling in prayer, praying on behalf of America. And I see legions from the God Star Sirius hearken to the prayers of the general. I see how the words spoken from his lips on that cold day in the wood were heard by the mighty blue eagle of Sirius, who responded instantaneously—these legions of light who made their way, encamping round about him and among the men and, by the infusion of that God-light, securing the victory.

America is the miracle of ascended-master love. America is a miracle land of violet fire; America is the victory of God's desire. America is the land of the abundance of the Mother flame! America is the land where the children of God are called home to the I AM name. America is the land where sons and daughters of God come forth to enshrine the noble purpose of God, of sacred worth. America is a land infused with sacred fire; America is born of God-desire.

I ask you then to secure the famous painting, a replica thereof, of George Washington kneeling in prayer. I ask that this shall be the sign of those who love America in Christ, in God, in freedom. I ask that you give this painting to your friends who are Christians, who are religious, who are devotees, that you ask them to have it in their homes, and that you ask them to pray with you for the light and the victory of America.

And above all I ask you, Keepers of the Flame, to kneel in prayer once a day with Godfre and with me before you retire and to remember to call for the victory of light in America and in the hearts of the American people. And I can assure you by all that lives and breathes, by all that is holy in love, the mighty blue eagle from Sirius will answer your call and will deliver this nation as one nation under God—individed, undivided, secure in the oneness of the light.

My vision is the vision of victory, and I will *speak* only of victory! I will *hear* only of victory! I will *see* only victory! I will *be* only victory! And do you know what I think? I think that mighty Victory will enlist me in his legions. [Audience laughs.] Would you not also enjoy being called forth to serve in those legions of Victory, being selected from among your peers by that mighty cosmic being who says to you: "Come with me! Your aura is the golden light of victory. The laurel wreath shines from you by your God-determination. I will enlist you in my hosts of light." That indeed is a privilege.

And I tell you, the hosts of light are oncoming! They are gathering as the legions of every archangel and cosmic being and Elohim. And if you could but see the glorious array, the demonstration, of these legions of light who will themselves march on Washington, D.C., on July 4 and 5, 1976, you would say to yourself: "I must be there! I must be among them, for I would be counted among those whose names will go down in cosmic history as the liberators of America! I must be the sword of the sacred Word and I must be the pen of truth. I must be the fire that ignites a world."

Whatever you will be for America, *be it to the utmost!* Be it to the fullest! Be it in the wholeness of the fire. Now I say, make your decision before the conclusion of this year—what you will be for America. And include a note to me as you pen your letters to the Lords of Karma and tell me what you will be for America, for I desire to be it with you. I desire to be in you and walk through you—Saint Germain, the Knight Commander! I would fulfill your dreams and your prayers, your longing for freedom. I would fulfill the law of love within you.

I stand before you to release the light of the violet flame for the filling-in of certain areas of the landed surface of America, certain areas on the astral plane and the mental plane that present a problem for the elementals and for hierarchy. I am releasing the light of my causal body to fill in the cracks and fissures in the land, to fill in those places where there has been experimentation with nuclear power within the earth.

I am filling in the fissures of consciousness, for I AM the balance of the nature kingdom. I AM the balance with God Tabor and Meru. I AM the balance with Cuzco and I AM the balance within you. So I am filling in the gaps, and I am filling in the crack of the Liberty Bell, and I am filling in the four lower bodies of all devotees who call to me.

This is the infilling light of the Holy Spirit, and the light of the violet flame is the light of the Holy Spirit for Aquarius. I place my flame in the amethyst crystal of the Mother that she might bear my flame and carry it forth by the power of the three-times-three—Morya's three dots, Lanello's three dots.

With a will to win and a flame of freedom, with the children of the Mother cheering her on, with the teaching of the Mother and the light of Gautama, how can we fail? We *shall* not! We will not! We will be victorious! Lo, because thou art, O God, I AM! I AM Sanctus Germanus within the heart of America, within the heart of a mother, within the heart of every Keeper of the Flame. Lo, I AM the victory of America in 1976! So be it!

VII

The Increment of Fire
by Sanat Kumara

In the light of the morning star I AM come! I come in the light of love. I come in the light of the Ancient of Days.[1] This is the I AM THAT I AM.[2] And the Lords of Flame are with me. We come from a meeting of the cosmic council where I stood so long ago and raised my hand in defense of Terra and her evolutions. I come from the deliberations of cosmic beings who have deigned to observe Terra and her evolutions and the light rays which mankind have invoked and the light rays which mankind have misqualified.

Now let the children of the sun hear my voice and hear my call! For when I volunteered to serve Terra aeons ago and this cosmic council accepted my offer to keep the flame of life, sons and daughters of God having evolved in this and these several systems of worlds volunteered to accompany me to Shamballa. Their vow was also accepted by this cosmic council, and by dispensation these sons and daughters were allowed to accompany me on that pilgrim journey to a darkened star.

I come then to earth this day to call to these sons and daughters of God who are yet abiding in time and space. I call to you who took your vow, you who remain

unascended because you have waited for the coming of
Lady Venus and for the fulfillment of her love. Now I say,
each one of you who remains—and I speak to you across
the face of the earth, in the cities and in the mountains, in
the country and in our ashrams of light—I say, come forth
to keep the flame of life! Forsake your entanglement with
the karmic yoke of Terra and the entanglement of human
creation and misqualification, the involvement with souls
who have compromised your light, who have strayed from
the Path. Come apart and be separate! [3]

I make this call because the cosmic council has
decreed that these very souls, the ones who accompanied
me, must rise in consciousness *this day*. It is imperative
that these souls who have the original flame of Sanat
Kumara rise to seize the responsibility which at times and
in certain embodiments they have let down.

And now I speak to the children of God who
responded to these sons and daughters when they came.
You who have seized that flame, you who have taken the
threefold flame at Shamballa from Gautama and from
Maitreya, you who have walked among those who were
counted as the saviours of mankind—I speak to you also;
for your names have been read by the Keeper of the Scrolls
before the cosmic council this day. And you are known
because you pledged your light to me, to Lady Venus, and
to the life of the evolutions of earth. *You* must rise this
day! You must return the flame on high and hold it high
as your Mother, the Goddess of Liberty, has showed you in
her presentation of that light to the world. You also must
rise this day! It is a mandate of the Lords of Flame and of
this cosmic council.

I speak, then, to a third group of souls who, seeing
the inner light of the original company, who, seeing the
light of those who responded to that company, have at
some point in time and space, even in this century,
determined to be keepers of the flame, who have determined to carry the torch of Liberty. To the originators,

to the preservers, and to those who would continue in
the love of the Buddhas, I come then with the mandate
of the cosmic council that all who have the awareness
of the threefold flame as the spark of life must receive in
this hour an increment of fire that will serve one of two
purposes, according to your will.

If you choose God and thereby choose to live as the
identity of God on earth, this increment of fire will
increase your God consciousness. If you choose the not-self
and rebellion and the forsaking of the flame and the vigil
of the Buddha and the Mother, then this increment of fire
will decrease your identity and your Self-awareness. For
this is the fiat of the Ancient of Days. To them that have
shall more be added; to them that have not shall be taken
away that which they have.[4]

I speak to you of the Lords of Sirius and the hierarchy
of the God Star, and I tell you the seriousness of coming
into the flame of the Great White Brotherhood. Over
thousands of years, there have been chelas who have
applied to the masters to receive a portion of the flame.
Therefore, unto every one of these who has petitioned the
Lord God, who has been received by an emissary of God,
ascended or unascended, who has received a portion—a
greater portion of the light of Shamballa than ordinary
mortals—unto you is passed a rod of fire that will touch
your heart at the conclusion of this dictation. And whether
you are here physically or elsewhere, the action that is to
take place will take place. And if you read of this
dispensation in the future—be it fifty or a hundred
years—you will know that at that very moment, if you
were counted among one of these three categories, you
received the increment of fire.

The increment of fire is an action of the judgment of
the law. The increment of fire, then, is the manifestation
of love to all who have come ahead of time to the Court of
the Sacred Fire, to the Lords of Karma, who have ahead of
time surrendered the not-self, who have confirmed all

vows of all ages, and who remain steadfast in the flame.
And to all who have remained steadfast in the teaching
given unto them by the teachers of the Great White
Brotherhood, so your steadfastness in the calling and your
obedience to the light will be the measure of the
increment of God-identity that will be sealed according to
the threefold flame within your heart.

This release of sacred fire comes, then, at a moment
when earth must rise a niche in the ladder of i-niche-
iation; and that ladder is a spiral of God consciousness.
Initiation is a timed action of the law. It is a moment when
infinity is manifest in time and space. And when the hour
of the initiation comes and mankind are not ready, they
fear it as they fear punishment or the Last Judgment. But
judgment, as initiation, is never punishment, but the
opportunity to know who you are and where you stand in
the cosmic hierarchy. And this also must be known by the
cosmic council who must yet deliberate the fate of Terra
and her evolutions.

When you receive the increment of sacred fire, you
will also receive the impelling of the Lords of Flame to
make secure in Mater an ever-expanding awareness of the
teaching. The teaching must live on! The teaching must be
secured in your heart. You must live for the teaching, and
all else must be put aside as useless timber. So if you would
be pillars in the temple of God and in the temple of
mighty Victory from Venus, [5] you must be forged by the
fire of the God Star. You must be useful timbers,
alabaster, and marble, and the light of crystal. You must
be crystallized in the God flame.

There is only one repository for light, and that is the
heart of the devotee unascended and of the masters
ascended. Therefore, to Terra and her evolutions comes
light! And what you *will* with selfhood will determine
what the light will define as identity within you. I raise my
hands over the earth for the release of the light of the
cosmic council; and when it shall go forth, it shall be for

the elevation of consciousness into the higher way. I commend you unto Christ, unto Buddha, unto your own I AM Presence, and to your victory by your steadfastness in the service of the messengers, of the hierarchy, and of your own soul's salvation. God be with you as you make your decision to be in the white-fire core or to be out!

I AM Sanat Kumara! I release the flame! And the rod of fire touches the hearts of those who know and keep the flame of life!

Comments by the Messenger Elizabeth Clare Prophet Following Sanat Kumara's Dictation

We will retire from the sanctuary in silence. I will bow to you at the door. And will you keep your meditation upon this fire as you visualize the earth and hold the balance for the adjustment and the alignment of the four lower bodies of the planet. There is an adjustment and a chemicalization in the four lower bodies of mankind by the release of the sacred fire. If you hold the harmony and keep the balance, the fire will be established and the earth will be raised.

Such increments of fire are necessary, but in the past they have often caused cataclysm. According to the ability of keepers of the flame to keep the flame, so will the disturbance in the elemental kingdom and in the four lower bodies be held at a minimum.

[On February 4 there was an earthquake in Guatemala and another in Arizona. Two more earthquakes struck Guatemala on February 6, bringing the death toll in Guatemala to more than 22,000. An earthquake occurred

off the west coast of Mexico on February 9. Such planetary upheaval and great loss of life can be averted in the
future only if the light-bearers on earth apply the teachings of the Great White Brotherhood and hold the balance
in the God flame as the light is accelerated for the age of
Aquarius.]

The sign of the heart, the head, and the hand to you.
May the peace of the Presence abide with you. Through
days of service and nights of rest, may the peace of the
Presence keep you blessed. The sign of the heart, the head,
and the hand. May the cosmic cross of white fire from the
heart of Jesus and Gautama, from the heart of Sanat
Kumara and Lady Master Venus and the cosmic council
and the Four and Twenty Elders, watch between thee and
me while we are absent one from the other and present
with our God.

Notes

Chapter I

1. 1 Pet. 2:5.
2. Rev. 16:14, 16; Acts 2:20.
3. Exod. 3:14.
4. Rev. 13:16-17.
5. Gen. 49; Rev. 7:4.

Chapter II

1. Rev. 12:1.
2. Jer. 31:33.
3. 1 Cor. 15:54.
4. Rom. 3:8.
5. Rev. 13:10.
6. John 16:24; Luke 11:9.
7. Matt. 2:16-18.
8. Matt. 5:15.
9. Luke 14:23.
10. Matt. 12:37.
11. Matt. 20:16.
12. See *Liberty Proclaims*, dictations by the Goddess of Liberty, published by The Summit Lighthouse.

Chapter III

1. Rev. 4:4.
2. Acts 10:34.
3. Eph. 5:26.

Chapter IV

1. 1 Sam. 15:22.
2. Matt. 5:48.
3. Rev. 4:4.
4. Matt. 12:25.
5. Rev. 12:1.

Chapter V

1. *There Is a Price to Pay for Chelaship*, 16 November 1975.
2. Matt. 16:18.
3. Rev. 12:1.

Chapter VI

1. Rev. 19:7; 21:9.
2. Rev. 21.
3. Matt. 19:26.

Chapter VII

1. Dan. 7:9.
2. Exod. 3:14.
3. 2 Cor. 6:17.
4. Matt. 13:12.
5. Rev. 3:12; Saint Germain, *Pearls of Wisdom*, 10 June 1960, pp. 2-3.

The Greater Way of Freedom

Tape recordings of these dictations,
including the messenger's lecture
given at this seminar,
are available on cassettes or reels.
For more information write
The Summit Lighthouse
Box A
Colorado Springs
Colorado 80901

You are invited
to study the teachings
of the ascended masters
published by The Summit Lighthouse
as *Pearls of Wisdom*
and sent to you
on a love-offering basis.
For information
write to:
The Summit Lighthouse
Box A
Colorado Springs
Colorado 80901

For information
on Summit University
write to:
Summit University
P.O. Box 1798
Colorado Springs
Colorado 80901